CARDINAL IS HER COLOR

CARDINAL IS HER COLOR

ONE HUNDRED FIFTY YEARS

OF ACHIEVEMENT AT

WILLIAM JEWELL COLLEGE

WILLIAM JEWELL COLLEGE
150 Years of Service
1849-1999

Book cover and interior design by Tim Lynch

Book publishing services by BookWorks Publishing, Marketing, Consulting

The William Jewell College Sesquicentennial Publications and Historical Research Committee would like to acknowledge with gratitude the able assistance of Pola Firestone of BookWorks in Overland Park, Kansas. The success of this publishing project owes much to her expertise, patience, persistence, and professionalism.

DEDICATION

Frank Hester, 1944-1996

Every great institution owes a measure of its greatness to those who have come before. At William Jewell College such names are legion. Their deeds and their spirits have left an indelible mark on the campus and on the world. That biblical "great cloud of witnesses" blesses indeed the Hill and their lives and accomplishments continue to inspire to present greatness. While dedicating this book to one individual, Frank Hester, the aim is to honor all those who have come before and helped make William Jewell the great school it is today.

Following a long family tradition, Frank Hester came to William Jewell in 1966 and graduated in 1969. Throughout the years he remained a loyal and active alum. Before his untimely death in August 1996, he was serving as co-chair of the sesquicentennial steering committee along with his wife, Juarenne.

To really know Frank Hester one must know something about the Phi Gamma Delta fraternity at William Jewell in the 1960s. I was a Sigma Nu. Like most of my Greek brothers (with our no-nonsense, Cheese Whiz-and-Ritz cracker midwest sensibilities) I tried to dismiss Frank and the "Fijis" with their convertibles, sleek wardrobes, insufferable wit and posh pretenses. If that was not enough, each spring they built a log wall around their fraternity house, dressed in island garb, and successfully squired every willing woman on campus into a weekend frenzy of stylized revelry—or so we thought. Our envy was palpable. The Fijis of the 1960s reached a zenith. They were what Frank Hester made them—sophisticated, enigmatic, charming, cultured, and marvelous fun!

After leaving William Jewell, Frank and I got on parallel tracks—living in Liberty and teaching in the Liberty school system. He was probably one of the most respected educators I have ever known. Everyone learned in Frank's social studies classes.

His students built things, discovered knowledge, learned respect and cultivated imaginations. Frank Hester gave his life to working with children. There is no higher calling.

Only his legendary devotion to and direction of Liberty's Clayview Country Club shadowed his reputation as a teacher. Single-handedly Frank forced the axis of Liberty's social universe straight through the Clayview swimming pool. Now a whole city became his fraternity. Whatever Frank touched he made fun. Entire generations of families will tell you that their days at Frank's pool were the best they have ever known.

Yet another great love of Frank's life was his city. As a city councilman, Frank defined the notion that Liberty could maintain its identity and heritage despite the suburban sprawl that often turns hometowns into shapeless bedroom housing divisions.

Frank demanded high-quality development, fastidious customer service, and a sense of community spirit from the city council. His vision earned him a cherished legacy—"City Father."

Though he loved his college, his fraternity and his city mightily, it was always people who came first with him. Frank Hester made the people and, in turn, the institutions he touched become special. William Jewell College, Liberty Public Schools, Clayview Country Club, Liberty, Mo.—all felt Frank's lasting mark. Most people are lucky to leave one legacy. Frank left four.

So many names and their accomplishments whisper on this hilltop campus. As the night breeze hangs on the great columns of Jewell Hall and the moonlight rests easily on the J Bench and Gano steps, another brother joins the march.

James W. "Jim" Dunn '71,
Liberty, Mo., 1998

FOREWORD

As William Jewell College commemorates its sesqui-centennial, it is an especially appropriate time to reflect on the tremendous impact this college has had on our region. When I think of William Jewell, I think of the thousands of young minds that have been molded there. I think of the hundreds of faculty members, administrators and trustees who have shown such admirable dedication to the college's mission and purposes. I think of the many residents of the greater Kansas City area who have been enriched by the vitality of its external programs.

Throughout its history William Jewell College has been an innovator in American education. The college and its leadership have always worked diligently to build its reputation as one of the best undergraduate liberal arts institutions in the midwest. Admirably, to complement its strong liberal arts foundation, William Jewell aims to instill in each student a sense of leadership, citizenship, ethics and spiritual values.

As a businessman and life-long resident of Kansas City, I find that my most indelible impression of William Jewell College is the interdependent relationship I observe between college and community. Established a year before the incorporation of Kansas City, the college is often referred to by the Kansas City Chamber of Commerce as the oldest "business" in continuous operation in the region. Moreover, it was for many years the only college available to educate the citizens of this metropolitan area.

Through the years, William Jewell alumni in the Kansas City area (now numbering over 6,000) have been instrumental in charting a better future for the city and the region.

Apart from the contributions of local alumni, the college plays a role in the lives of thousands of area residents and helps mold the cultural fabric of the region through its incomparable Fine Arts series. Each spring and fall, the college presents outstanding performances, ranging from such notables as Luciano Pavarotti and Itzhak Perlman to the Royal Shakespeare Company and the Russian National Ballet.

In the following chapters of *Cardinal Is Her Color*, you will relive the triumphs and challenges of William Jewell history, with particular emphasis on the post-World War II years. The chapters do not flow chronologically; rather, they are organized according to subject matter. Each segment is composed in a unique style, featuring a very personal voice by individuals who hold Jewell close to their hearts. You will see important bits and pieces of Jewell history through the eyes of those who have been there.

As you might expect, the final chapter encourages all college friends and constituents to confront the future and the dawning of a new millennium. Most of us would agree that there is no greater challenge than preparing future generations to assume their roles in society. I believe William Jewell College has the vision and the will, the people and the programs, to succeed in this all-important endeavor.

Donald J. Hall, Chairman
Hallmark Cards, Inc.

CONTENTS

ALMA MATER

Cardinal is her color,
Jewell is her name.
high upon a hill she stands
And we will fight to keep her fame.
Loyalty, Allegiance, Alma Mater true,
We will love thee, serve thee forever
William Jewell.

William Jewell College,
Far her fame is known.
Deep within our hearts she dwells
And there our love for her has grown.
Cardinal teams are warriors,
Bold and brave and true.
We will love thee, praise thee forever
William Jewell.

Christian faith and vision
By her founders made
The cause of her existence
And the bounty for which they prayed.
Working, trusting, onward,
God will bless our school.
We will love thee, praise thee forever
William Jewell.

The Alma Mater

The tune and first stanza of the *Alma Mater* beloved by generations of Jewell students was composed by John (Jack) Wilkes '42. Wilkes penned the melody and lyrics while traveling to Syracuse, New York, for the Christmas holiday break in December of 1938. David Grosch, professor of music from 1928 to 1955, was enthusiastic about the work Wilkes had created, but believed the song was too short to properly sing Jewell's praises. He convinced Wilkes to augment the original material, which he did with the assistance of Biron Bush '40. They wrote the song's second stanza just before it was presented in chapel in the fall of 1939. Following that well-received performance, the *Alma Mater* was adopted by the Student Council as the official song of William Jewell College.

When a marching band was instituted at Jewell by Professor Ed Lakin in the 1950s, a multi-part instrumental arrangement was needed. Professor Lakin, a respected music faculty member from 1950 to 1977, did a full orchestration and four-part arrangement of the *Alma Mater*. That arrangement has been featured at countless William Jewell events over the past five decades. A coda to the *Alma Mater* story was added in the 1980s, when Bush attended an alumni function at which the song was played and realized there was no mention of the College's Christian heritage in the lyrics. He added a third stanza which speaks of the founders' "Christian faith and vision."

CHAPTER 1

HISTORY of WILLIAM JEWELL

Jewell Is Her Name

by David O. Moore

*W*illiam Jewell College resulted from the vision of Baptists who lived along the Missouri River, a watery highway across the state. In the late 1830s, four persons set their minds to developing an education institution for the training of young ministers and laymen. They were Thomas Fristow, Ebinezer Rogers, Fielding Wilhoit, and a young physician, late of Little Bonne Femme church, named William Jewell. These four, like the Four Horsemen of the Apocalypse, swept among the churches of the Missouri River valley encouraging and proposing "a college among us."

This achievement was slow and arduous. A decision to establish a college and accept Dr. Jewell's handsome grant of 3,951 acres of river bottomland, worth more than $10,000, came to naught for failure to secure other monies. But in

Dr. William Jewell

1847, renewed effort was expended. By 1848, $16,000 had been raised with great hopes for more. Hence, the General Association (forerunner of the Missouri Baptist Convention) approved a proposal to ask the state legislature for a charter, and a unique one was granted and signed by the governor on February 27, 1849. With this, a college was born.

William Jewell College is the lengthened shadow of six persons: Dr. William Jewell, its founder; Alexander Doniphan, its philanthropist; Thomas Rambaut, its academician; John Priest Greene, its father confessor; John Herget, its solidifier; and Walter Pope Binns, its prophet of the post-war years.

H.I. Hester, the legendary professor of religion, has adequately told the early history in two books. His *Jewell Is Her Name* covers definitively the first

William Jewell
College Seal of
1928

100 years, and a small monograph brings the story to 1979. This present account, therefore, accedes to these records and emphasizes the last fifty years, 1949-1999.

ENTERING THE POST-WAR YEARS

The person who ushered the college into the post-war years, who gave it the base for its modern achievement as a school of "considerable respect among small institutions of higher learning," was Walter Pope Binns. He became president July 1, 1943, and served the second longest tenure of any president, nineteen years.

Binns was a Georgian by birth but a Virginian by demeanor and style. A tall, stately man, he had eyes which measured a person keenly, if they saw the person at all. Buried in reflective thought, he might pass a friend on the sidewalk with no memory of ever seeing that friend. It soon became commonplace to say, "William Jewell is a college of cardinals and has a pope for a president." A genteel man, mild of manner until ruffled, Binns cast an image of aristocratic aloofness. This was not so, however. He was no aristocrat, but was a Southern gentleman, soul and body. His was a tender heart and he always said it troubled him deeply to have to dismiss some student for disciplinary reasons. "I have children, too, you know," he would say.

Binns was married to Blanche Roberta Mallary of Macon, Ga. No more gracious hostess and first

lady ever presided at "the president's mansion." She spoke gently in her Southern accent while grace, mingled with charm, flowed from her. She was chosen "Mother of Missouri" in 1959.

President Binns assumed his role at a propitious time. He, with the trustees, must see the college through the closing war years, must prepare for the return of war veterans and other students and lay plans also for the second century of the college's existence. Goals growing out of plans for the centennial celebration included strengthening the liberal arts program of the college, stabilizing enrollment at 500 students, and raising funds of $3,870,750 for endowment purposes. A curricular program organized around twelve departments was envisioned, each of which was to be endowed with $250,000.

With the influx of students from 1946-1949, led mainly by GIs, the enrollment mushroomed to 700, not the limited 500 set earlier. Making room for students who desired admission to the school always overshadowed enrollment restrictions. By the 1980s, enrollment would rest beyond 1,450 full-time day-school students with some 200-250 additional evening students. Students were revenue, and qualified applicants were seldom placed on waiting lists even when living quarters were full.

The goal of twelve endowed departments was Binns' hope. It was not reached; but six were funded as planned. Great success was achieved in providing buildings to accommodate the burgeoning student body. Jewell's present campus largely took shape in these years. Old Ely was demolished to open the quad aesthetically. The following new buildings were constructed: Greene Hall, for administration; Jones Hall, a women's residency; Luther Greene stadium; Eaton Hall, a men's residency; and Yates College Union. Plans for the present library building were set in motion as well.

Dr. Binns was a forthright administrator, quick of mind and quick of decision. He might step across the hall for a short chat with Dr. Hester but when he returned he often knew his decision. A spring ritual for all faculty was the granting of contracts for the following year. There was no tenure. However, on occasion, when a young prospective teacher raised the issue, Dr. Binns informed him, "Yes, we have tenure. You all have tenure. If your work is satisfactory, you can remain as long as you desire. Of course, unsatisfactory work will always bring termination."

But Binns was an honorable and just man. He used a yellow, legal-sized "lawyer's pad" to list the teachers and the salary offer he proposed for each. He and

Minetry Jones, college business manager, had previously worked these amounts out. A teacher would arrive at the office, be seated and watch Dr. Binns scan the listing. Looking up through his pinched-nose spectacles, Dr. Binns would begin.

"Well, Mr. Rose, you've had a good year here with us. I hope you have enjoyed it. We appreciate our fine teachers and because of your efforts, I'm

Old Ely

going to pay you $300 more next year. That will make you $5,700, paid over ten months." He would pause, pick up the contract and hand it over. Then he would close with, "What do you think of that? That's good, isn't it?"

Usually, matters ended there and the professor would take the contracts, sign one for Binns and one for the dean and keep one for himself. The experience was daunting. An occasion the writer remembers clearly. He entered the office, and after the usual banter, President Binns scanned his pad, raised his eyes, and began. "Well, sir, you've had an exceptional year-no problems. (A most unusual achievement for that professor!) I want to show that we appreciate your work and I'm going to give you a $2,500 raise for next year."

The writer caught his breath. Two thousand five hundred dollars, a 33 percent increase in salary. Had the millennium arrived? The contracts were handed over and signed on the spot. Ecstasy reigned on the walk back to Jewell Hall. Having called his wife with the news, the professor rocked back and forth in his chair. Life was just, after all.

Then the phone rang. "Binns here," the voice said. "Please come back to my office and bring your contract with you." Click! The professor froze. "Bring the contract," he had said.

In the president's office, Binns seemed quietly perturbed. He was uncertain how to proceed. "I'm embarrassed," he said. "I made a mistake on your contract. When I looked down at the pad, I quoted you the figure for the professor right under yours. Please give me back your contract and we'll correct it. Your raise is $400." Dejected, the professor handed it over. Crestfallen, and a little bit sore, he made his way back to his office. Slowly, he dialed his home and said, "Honey, I hope you haven't bought that new dress yet. We didn't get that big raise."

Then he just sat in his chair-no rocking, no humming, no saying life is fair. The telephone rang. "Binns here," from the voice on the other end. "Bring your contract and please come back to my office. I need to see you." Click! The professor looked down at the sheet of typed paper. I'll be dad-blamed if I take another whack off my salary," he exploded. "This is too much."

Back in Binns' office a gracious, almost repentant fellow greeted the teacher. "Sit down, sir, I owe you an apology. I should not have done to you what I did. It was my mistake and I'm just going to stick by my original statement. Here's the original contract, $2,500 intact. Give me the one you are holding and I'll tear it up. I'm sorry for what has happened." The professor left the office smiling and resolute. He had met a good man, not too proud to confess a mistake and set it right.

President Binns felt that he, acting by and through trustee authority, led the college. He protected, defended, advanced and honored his school. Although professors sometimes felt that Binns was aloof from them, he always protected them from outside criticism or unjust attack. But he expected dedicated achievement from each. He was unswerving in his expectation that faculty and staff should act according to the stated Christian ideals of the college. These included a clear realization by all that Jewell was a Baptist institution, although not a narrow, sectarian one.

Dr. Binns introduced a summer study program for professors after they had been at the school for three or more years. He was the authorizer and decision-maker of these grants. After a religion professor had been approved for one of these grants, he was in the president's office shortly before departure for Union Theological Seminary in New York City. There the president, with not a hint of a smile, addressed him. "I'm glad you're going to Union for study. A professor needs to keep fresh in his teaching. But listen to me now. Don't you go up there to that Northern school and get any new ideas. We like you here just the way you are." One has to interpret this to mean that Binns eschewed any taint of theological liberalism. It must not, however, be seen to mean he was a present-day fundamentalist. He respected others' theological views and granted their right to independent interpretation.

His friend, former student colleague, and for eighteen years his vice president, Dr. H. I. Hester, writes of Binns, "His administration was one of the most fruitful of any in the long history of the college." These two had led in the formation of the

Association of Southern Baptist Colleges and Schools in 1948. They traveled together to national meetings, played Rook together (Binns always choosing Hester for partner), made visits of condolences to student families in times of crisis, and thought through college problems together until June 30, 1961. Hester then left the college to become vice president of Midwestern Baptist Theological Seminary, where Millard Berquest, one of Hester's former students, was president.

On February 28, 1962, President Binns announced his impending retirement. Now sixty-five years old, he judged it time to move on. *The Kansas City Star* said editorially, "Today, William Jewell is one of the excellent smaller colleges of the Middle West. Under the direction of Dr. Binns its educational services have been strengthened. It has continued its devotion to Christian philosophy. The growing college at Liberty will always owe him a special debt of gratitude."

At this point in the life of the school, things were bright indeed. Enrollment stood at 1,012, a peak. New buildings surrounded the quad. Kansas City public relations were at an all-time high. A grant from the Ford Foundation of $183,500 had been received, income from which was to be used for improvement of faculty salaries. But ominous clouds hung across the horizon.

Student unrest, national and local, was developing. The divisive spirit of Vietnam affected everyone. There was little participation by students or

William Jewell College Seal of 1942

faculty in policy-making procedures on campus. A national trend toward granting faculty tenure as a guarantor of academic freedom had not yet reached Jewell. Further, faculty had become restive about denominational relations with Missouri Baptists, and a pro-Baptist versus non-denominational schism developed. Against this backdrop, the search for a new president was on.

FACING A CHANGED SOCIAL CULTURE

A trustee nominating committee was appointed by its president, Charles F. Curry, who was to serve as its chairman. In their efforts, two Kansas City churches came to the fore. Curry and several strong board members were in Calvary Baptist Church, while Mr. Will Browning and an active contingent were at Wornall Road Church. The first choice for president was the Reverend Conrad Willard, immediate past pastor of Calvary Baptist. Following an interview with the full faculty at the college, however, Willard withdrew his name.

President H. Guy Moore

This opened the way for the selection of the Reverend H. Guy Moore, who had previously been in consideration, and who had been pastor at Wornall Road. Browning was a supporter of Moore, his former pastor, and in the end Moore was chosen. He was pastor of Broadway Baptist Church, Ft. Worth, Texas, and had no prior experience in educational administration. He assumed his role in June, 1962, and served until August 31, 1968.

Dr. Moore was a man with a pastor's heart who found no zest in day-to-day decisions that required dismissals or remonstrances with staff. He longed for positions and decisions to be worked out in community fashion where consensus was achieved. This style of decision-making was a marked contrast to that of Binns. From the beginning, however, the new president was liked by the faculty, which set about strengthening its role in administrative matters that related to academic affairs. A restless student body also sought, and secured, more input in college administration. Progress was made on a tenured faculty program, and both students and faculty became more involved with college governance.

President Moore put into motion approval for faculty to elect and develop an effective faculty steering committee (later called Faculty Council). The first members of this committee were David O. Moore, Wes Forbis, Douglas Harris, Georgia Bowman, and Marvin Dixon. Its role and work for the college was steadily refined and developed until it had a meaningful place in academic budget preparation and allocation, selection of new faculty, evaluation of faculty for merit pay raises, and consideration for tenure, when this was finally approved. The North Central Association of Colleges and Secondary Schools, an accrediting agency, supported this move.

During the Moore administration four major building projects were completed. Construction of the library building was finished in the summer of 1965. A new wing was added to Semple Hall, and the Yates College Union nearly doubled in size. Browning Hall, a new residence facility for men, was constructed on a site just west of Eaton Hall.

In the midst of these things, key staff decisions had to be made. The academic dean, Garland Taylor, left for a similar position at Mercer University in Georgia. Dr. Bruce Thomson was chosen as replacement. The esteemed physical education department director and head football coach, Dr. Norris Patterson, took a position at United States International University in San Diego, Calif. At one point, student involvement rose to fever pitch when two faculty members were disciplined for improper classroom demeanor. The trustees subsequently placed them on terminal leave, with pay for one year. Mass student protest, covered by Kansas City television, served to heighten concerns about presidential leadership. When student enrollment and institutional fund raising did not measure up to trustee expectations, further dissatisfaction surfaced. As a partial corrective, a trustee decision to establish a position of director of development was made.

On February 20, 1967, it was reported to a trustee committee that E. Lee McLean had been selected to serve as a consultant on establishing a development program for the college. McLean later recommended B.G. Olson for this position, and Olson was elected as executive vice president and director of development in October of 1967.

Over time, Olson's emerging powers overshadowed those of the president, a fact which a North Central accrediting team pointed out in a site visit in the spring of 1968. For this and other reasons the college was placed on a three-year private probation, with another review slated at the end of that period.

President Moore ultimately left the college at the end of August in 1968. He returned to his first love, a pastorate of the New Plymouth Baptist Church in Alexandria, Va. Olson was named acting president, but his administrative style did not prove to be a good fit for William Jewell. By September 1969, Olson had sought employment at a school near Chicago and was gone from the campus.

Trustees were busy during 1969 searching out their next president while Dr. E.W. Holzapfel was acting president. Mr. Will Yates, patriarch of trustees, used his considerable clout insisting that the president be a respected Missouri Baptist pastor. In the search, attention turned to Dr. Thomas W. Field, past president of the Missouri Convention of Baptists and pastor of First Baptist Church in Springfield.

A PLOTTED COURSE FOR SUPERIOR ACADEMICS

At a board meeting in Kansas City, May 2, 1970, Dr. Field was unanimously chosen. He immediately accepted. But it was no "cake walk" to which he had been called. Fewer than 850 students were expected that fall. A deficit in the operating budget of $295,000-$350,000 was projected. Full accreditation had still not been received and faculty morale was low, with some openly expressing resistance to another "Baptist preacher-type" for president. But Field loved the challenge.

He came with enthusiasm, a salesman's personality, the ability to analyze difficult problems, and a willingness to delegate responsibility. He was no academician and lacked experience working directly with faculty. This he delegated to his academic dean. When a problem arose with business management, he made changes that brought "his team" together. Dr. Bruce Thomson, who had been academic dean, was moved to business affairs and the associate dean, Gordon Kingsley, became full dean. Both moves proved strokes of keen insight.

Primary problems were twofold: to build the student enrollment and to regain full accreditation. President Field attacked the first of these at the point of his greatest strength, his popularity and recognition among Baptist pastors. He offered as many as one hundred "Presidential Grants" to students who could qualify for admission and were recommended by their pastor. These grants carried full tuition remission. Thirty-seven were accepted the first fall, 1970. Dr. Field then instituted his "Church and Campus Award" for qualified students, each carrying a $1,000 grant toward tuition. In 1970, 906 students were enrolled, and in 1972 enrollment had grown to 1,199. By 1972, the college was able to close its fiscal year with a surplus of $25,000, due primarily to Field's aggressive action.

The second major issue was accreditation. Faculty and students joined in this effort. The accrediting agency examination would be in the spring of 1971. Therefore, revision of curriculum, strengthening of organizational structure, with a faculty statement of purpose, all had to be addressed. From these efforts came a new curriculum, named "Achievement '70s: Education for Individual Achievement." It featured a new school calendar, called a 4-1-4 plan. These were the products of Dr. Kingsley's prolific and creative mind but were carried through by earnest faculty.

Because of the unified effort of many, the trustee report in May, 1971, documented a most encouraging team visit by the North Central Association. Dr. Bohm, of that team, commended "the instructional organization of the curriculum, the unusually high caliber of teaching techniques" and stated that the four science departments were "of uniquely high caliber and markedly superior to most private liberal arts colleges." President Field was optimistic. He felt the reaction of the review team was positive and in the college's favor. At the September meeting of the trustees, he reported officially: The college had regained a full ten-year accreditation. The sanction of a former time had been lifted and one of Field's best achievements was secured.

President Field had managed to secure the enthusiastic support of the trustees and neutralize some of the "factionalism" which had existed in prior years. Repeatedly, they commended their president and his staff for growth plus the spirit of aggressive change toward better academics at William Jewell. They were pleased with the general tranquility that existed. As a result of this, improvement of physical properties could be accomplished. Renovation of older buildings, the erection of new ones, and the attractive beautification of the entire campus ensued.

By 1980, the "Decade of Achievement" drew to a close. The college had made provision for study, by selected students and faculty, at Harlaxton College in Grantham, England. Its Fine Arts Series had acquired national recognition. Growth of the student body was constant and planned. Faculty was steadily engaged in review, development, and possible change of its instructional processes. A fully integrated program of sabbatical leaves was in force. Students were represented on all important administrative and faculty committees. The first half of Charles Dickens' famous statement applied: "It was the best of times."

In the year preceding Dr. Field's sixty-fifth birthday, faculty and others began raising the question of his possible retirement. They were concerned since the Field tenure had been very successful and since securing a new administrator always carried a degree of uncertainty. At this time, Dean Kingsley had accepted an offer to go to Mercer University in Macon, Ga., where he would also serve as dean. Faculty became greatly concerned as to how events might unfold.

President Field had elevated Kingsley to the academic deanship, had worked cooperatively with him in developing innovative programs, and was genuinely proud of his accomplishments. Faculty also had very high regard for Kingsley and did not wish to lose his constructive leadership. In the spring of 1978, when the Kingsley departure was imminent, the faculty council met cautiously. They asked whether Kingsley might be a good choice as president of William Jewell.

One member was selected to approach Kingsley first and secured Kingsley's affirmation that he was interested in staying at Jewell. The next move was to approach the president, who, on being invited, was pleased to have a steak luncheon with the council in the Union building. He was told, with utter sincerity, of faculty appreciation for his leadership at Jewell and of their deep feeling concerning rumors that he soon might retire. The council reminded the president of how they respected Kingsley and regretted his plan to move to another

William Jewell College Shield of 1960

9

school. Since Field had encouraged, somewhat groomed, and always supported Kingsley, they asked if he would consider suggesting to the board that Kingsley be chosen as president-elect, to take office when Field had completed his tenure. To do this would seem to be one way of ensuring continuation of the plans, hopes, and achievements for the school President Field had come to love and for which he had done so much.

Two friends who, as presidents, moved the college forward dramatically: Dr. J. Gordon Kingsley & Dr. Thomas S. Field

President Field was gracious and open to the proposal. He considered the implications and reported soon to the council his decision to approach the trustees suggesting that they mutually work on the proposal. This they did and on May 1, 1978, the trustees made Kingsley president-elect. He continued to serve as academic dean until President Field's retirement, which occurred June 30, 1979.

A gala retirement affair was planned and executed for the Fields, who were celebrated for their significant achievements at William Jewell. July 1 marked the beginning of the Kingsley era.

TIME FOR VISION AND DREAMS

The new president moved easily into his official duties. Dr. Kingsley was the first president since the 1800s to rise from the ranks of the teaching profession. He had participated in or planned all of the academic changes for the last ten years. The college he inherited was poised for a surge of new development and he used all of his imaginative skills, his remarkable ability as a public speaker, and his mastery with words for the advancement of the college.

Everywhere on campus it became evident that Britain had come to Clay County. After a while a red double-decker bus came to campus. The president was seen in a black London taxi shipped in from the Isles. A red telephone kiosk appeared at the front of Brown Hall. British decorative flags hung from special masts and "British speak" was the norm. One of the new president's masterful sermons was built around his spiritual epiphany while viewing the massive and moving interior of Durham cathedral in North England. The college loved it. Greater Kansas City was impressed. It was still "the best of times."

Kingsley inherited a student body of 1,450 and a faculty of eighty-three. A second ten-year extension of full accreditation by North Central had just been received. It gave glowing praise for faculty, saluted the spirit of the student body, and spoke highly of both staff and the board of trustees. There was a slight caution that "much work remained for the board in the area of development." Arises that 'cursed sprite,' the financial development aspect again. It would not go away.

The new president pressed ahead, through his faculty dean, with his academic dreams. A team-taught, interdisciplinary program of general education called "Foundations for the Future" came off the drawing board. What was called an Oxbridge Tutorial Program, named for both Oxford and Cambridge universities in Britain, was proposed, modified, and finally instituted in 1983. Efforts were rewarded. A grant of $1,050,000 was given by the Hall Family Foundations dedicated to supporting this highly individualized program of study, a year of which was to be spent in Britain.

There was activity on all sides. Brown Gymnasium was completely rebuilt on the inside with a challenge grant from the Mabee Foundation of $450,000. It became a combination office and teaching complex for art and psychology plus a small theater for fine arts. A Center for Baptist Historical Studies was created and housed in the special collections section of the library. Kingsley, himself a Ph.D. in religious history, pushed for this program, which received financial aid from the Missouri Baptists and a sizable bequest from William Partee of Hannibal, Mo.

A campaign for enlarging the endowment and for building a new science complex as well as rebuilding the interior of Marston Hall was planned and executed. This project was aided by a handsome gift given by Mr. and Mrs. John White of Massachusetts. Both were former students at

William Jewell and John White later became chair of the trustees. The campaign was a magnificent success. More than $27 million was raised. White Science Center now stands east of Marston connected to it by walkway and elevator. The old Marston Hall was reconfigured for classrooms and offices for faculty and staff.

President Kingsley, center, joined by Adele and Don Hall, good friends of William Jewell.

In this remarkable decade, 1980-1990, Luciano Pavarotti received an honorary degree from Jewell and sang a brilliant gala benefit concert at the Music Hall, Kansas City. Other notables followed in the Fine Arts Series. *U.S. News & World Report* gave William Jewell positive rankings in its editions of "America's Best Colleges."

Kingsley may have dreamed of his college as an Athens on the Missouri, a Harvard of the midwest, an Oxford in the New World. He closed a report to the trustees once by saying this may be the "year of transition from being a good college to becoming a great one." Indeed, he pushed relentlessly toward that goal. Six task forces, comprised of Kansas City area community leaders, faculty, staff and students, had been at work on a Commission On the Future, which was ultimately to recommend an "Agenda for Excellence, 2000."

Always the faculty's friend, Kingsley worked constantly for increased compensation, while he demanded steady development of teaching skills. A study of salary structures conducted by independent researchers Dr. Thomas Emmet and Dr. John Minter gave praise to William Jewell for progress in this area. The president envisioned a Hall of Fame for faculty, which came to pass, and was added, in portraiture, to the Yates College Union.

President Kingsley teaches a seminar in English Literature.

Student enrollment remained relatively steady throughout the years 1987 to 1994, reaching 1,477 in 1991. Kingsley praised the admission staff for its achievements. Everywhere on campus, students were directly involved in matters of college life, serving on faculty committees, administrative and staff study reviews, and in their own student senate efforts. The president wrote, in a trustee report, "It is my 20th year of service with William Jewell College in some capacity and it is a fine little school I have come to love very much."

But the director of development position was vacant again. It had been a continuing problem ever since the Olson fiasco. In 1986, Dr. Richard B. Lancaster, lately of Simpson, Beloit and Earlham Colleges, resigned his responsibility in this area of development after slightly more than one year. There was constant shuffling of the director of

alumni affairs. By 1988, a complete reorganization of staff positions occurred, fueled by concern about fund raising.

Larry Stone became development, public relations, alumni and admissions supervisor; Suzanne Patterson assumed the development position; Ed Leonard, alumni affairs; Ed Norris, admissions; and Charlotte Legg, public relations. They were a good team, but other opportunities beckoned. By 1995, all of these administrators had left the college.

President Binns, in another time, began Achievement Day in Kansas City by asking the question: "What is a college?" His reply to his own question was unduly simplistic, but the question was of utmost importance. As the Kingsley era at Jewell approached its end, some of the answer to Binns' question was being offered.

Colleges thrive, grow, and survive on zeal-stirring tradition and alumni loyalty. The Jewell kind of school depended also on its denominational commitment. To be a Baptist college was desirable. Colleges also succeed on account of the fertile minds of faculty, their teaching skill and, in this case, their enthusiasm for combining Christian ideals and liberal arts. Dr. Earl McGrath, consultant to the college in the early Kingsley period, made clear that small colleges remain good, or become excellent, through clear perceptions and statements of their mission. They had to rigorously hold to these.

The legacy of the Kingsley administration was a

strong one. The endowment had been significantly enhanced as a result of the successful $27 million Leadership 2000 campaign. The physical plant was renewed with construction of the new $7.5 million White Science Center and a completely refurbished Marston Hall. Programmatically, Kingsley's inspired vision of combining the British tutorial system with the American approach to higher education may be his most enduring legacy. The Oxbridge Honors Program which he conceived continues to attract some of the country's best and brightest college students to William Jewell.

As Dr. Ann Marie Shannon, the first senior tutor of the Oxbridge program, put it: "Dr. Kingsley is the person who imagined Oxbridge into being. It's an example of what I think of as his creative imagination. William Jewell is a different, stronger, better college because of him."

After the board of trustees began to have differences with the president over leadership and administrative philosophy, Dr. Kingsley retired from the college in October 1993. Following the interim presidency of Dean Jim E. Tanner during the 1993-94 academic year, Dr. W. Christian Sizemore was named the institution's thirteenth president.

"Chris" Sizemore was well prepared for his Jewell presidential role. He had spent eleven years as president of Alderson-Broaddus College in West Virginia, in addition to a stint as a teaching faculty member at Southeastern Baptist Seminary. He had

served on the faculty, as acting president, dean, and librarian, at South Georgia College, in addition to service at Florida State University and the University of North Carolina. Earned degrees of Ph.D., B.D., M.L.S., and B.A. each prepared him for the task at hand. His administrative skills were honed during additional study at the Institute for Educational Management of Harvard University.

Among the first priorities of Sizemore's presidency was the installation of a computer network to allow students and faculty access to the vast resources of the information superhighway. In his inaugural address, Sizemore noted: "William Jewell acknowledges that technology is increasingly important to our present and our future. Institutions of quality cannot ignore and must incorporate the tools of technology and communications in order to meet the challenges of our rapidly changing global community."

When Sizemore took office in the fall of 1994, computer use on the Jewell campus was spotty at best, with only about 10 percent of the college community receiving institutional support for access to the burgeoning field of information technology. Within a year, the college was fully networked, linked by more than 1,600 computer access points.

William Jewell has achieved much broader recognition and visibility during the tenure of Chris and Anne Sizemore. Both are heavily involved in civic and charitable activities in Liberty and Kansas City. Also, both are well respected for their service to church and educational associations at the state and national level.

Internet access brought with it the ability to connect with national and international databases, transforming the way students and faculty approached research and learning. With the introduction of e-mail addresses, faculty and staff could communicate more effectively on campus as well. The college's web site went on-line in January of 1996, providing alumni, friends, and prospective students with worldwide access to current information.

With the successful networking project behind him, Sizemore moved to other initiatives. The board of trustees was strengthened and diversified with the addition of Kansas City civic leaders and alumni, as well as business and professional leaders from outside the Baptist denomination. The board welcomed its first African-American member, and faculty and student representatives were added to various trustee committees.

In the arena of strategic planning, Sizemore initiated the most extensive self-study in the history of the college and began charting a course that would take William Jewell into the next millennium. Strategic planning became the major college initiative of both the 1995-96 and 1996-97 academic years. Sizemore's charge was to connect the strengths of the past with the possibilities of the future, always adapting to the changing circumstances of a technology-driven society.

"We must have a thoughtful plan in order to succeed, even to survive as a quality institution," Sizemore told the strategic planning steering committee, which included trustees, faculty, administrators, staff, students, alumni, and community members.

Dr. Ann Marie Shannon was recruited to guide the strategic planning process internally. The steering committee engaged in an extensive data-gathering process drawing from both internal and external sources to learn how Jewell was perceived by various groups. Based on those findings, the committee identified an institutional core of values and then assessed "opportunities" and "threats."

Market research revealed that the community perceived William Jewell to be an institution positioned to prepare leaders who are able to work in teams; who are self-directed and adaptable to change; and who possess skills sharpened in an environment that purposefully connects the liberal arts with professional capabilities. The data-gathering process allowed the committee to reaffirm the three basic tenets of William Jewell's mission:

> *To provide students a liberal arts education of superior quality;*
>
> *To serve communities beyond the campus educationally, culturally, and socially;*
>
> *To be an institution loyal to the ideals of Christ, demonstrating a Christian philosophy for the whole of life, and expressing the Missouri Baptist heritage which is the foundation of the college.*

Additional outgrowths of the strategic planning process included the initiation of an integrated marketing and communications program. A new, cabinet-level position was created at the college to oversee new initiatives in this area. Efforts to sharpen Jewell's institutional identity were enhanced by means of a redesigned logo and a comprehensive graphic standards program that enabled all college communications to speak with a clear and consistent voice. Public relations and marketing efforts were directed to a much broader audience. The planning and budgeting process was revised and strengthened, with spending decisions tied to priorities established through broad consensus.

Other highlights of the Sizemore administration included the following:

• The development office was stabilized and energized under the guidance of vice president for institutional advancement Thad Henry. Henry brought in a staff with strong professional credentials and restructured the office to give greater focus to annual giving, planned giving, corporate-foundation support, and major gifts. Under his leadership the "New Century" campaign was initiated, representing the most ambitious capital fundraising effort in college history.

• Large endowment gifts supported continued excellence in academics. The Pryor Leadership Studies Program received start-up funding and then a generous $1.2 million endowment from alumni Fred and Shirley Pryor. Five endowed academic chairs were added–two in biology and one each in mathematics, religion and physics-at $1 million each. The Service Learning Program institutionalized Jewell's long-standing service ethic, thanks to the generosity of an anonymous donor who provided a $1.5 million gift. Also, an estate bequest from alumni Van and Vernalee Pearson provided more than $2 million for academic scholarships and support of tennis. Jewell's overall athletic program received a major infusion of support to allow expanded opportunities for female student-athletes, and a completely restructured general education program brought an interdisciplinary approach to the liberal arts curriculum.

• In terms of bricks and mortar, the Sizemore years were active as well. A new entrance provided a more welcoming gateway to the campus. A multi-million dollar Greek residential complex offered an innovative partnership between the college and its Greek-letter organizations. A new, Olympic-caliber track was constructed around Patterson Field, bearing the name of principal donor Garnett Peters III. The President's Home underwent a major renovation that allows the residence to serve more effectively as the "front door" of the campus in entertaining alumni and guests. Preliminary plans were completed for renovation of Jewell Hall, Gano Chapel, and Yates College Union as part of the aforementioned New Century campaign, whose kickoff coincided with the sesquicentennial celebration.

William Jewell College Logo of 1971

William Jewell College Logo of 1980

WILLIAM JEWELL COLLEGE

*William Jewell
College Logo of
1997*

Dr. W. Christian Sizemore

"Our research results are clear," Sizemore told the campus community following the 1997 report of the strategic planning committee. "William Jewell is currently known regionally as an outstanding liberal arts college. Building on that reputation and the resources at hand, I believe that the college is positioned to move into the national arena of liberal arts colleges. It is toward this end that our resources must be directed."

With a renewed commitment to the college's mission, the William Jewell community stands ready to build on the strengths of the past and move forcefully into the twenty-first century. To paraphrase the words of historian L.M. Dawson writing about Jewell for the Missouri Baptist Historical Society: "With such powerful advocates, with so grand a cause, and with so receptive a community, failure hardly seems possible."

CHAPTER 2

CHRISTIAN HERITAGE

Christian Faith and Vision

by Doran McCarty

*T*he heritage of an institution gives it soul. The Christian heritage of William Jewell College is a great part of her distinguished history and a vibrant part of her continuing mission.

William Jewell's history is deeply rooted in the Baptist tradition. An understanding of how this relationship first began, and then developed through the years, is vital to understanding the Jewell story.

Soon after the formation of a statewide Baptist organization in 1834, a handful of laymen began to see the need for a Baptist college to provide a higher level of training for church ministers and lay leaders. Their primary concern was to ensure the progress of the new state organization. It took some time, but as more and more Baptists around the state stepped forward to pledge support for a new college, Jewell's formal and lasting affiliation with Missouri Baptists began.

Through the years, this affiliation has become ever more sharply defined. As citizens of a Civil War border state, Missourians were divided in their sympathies between the North and the South.

These divisions remained long after the war's end in 1865, especially among Baptists who maintained ties to both the Northern and Southern Baptist Conventions. As a result, Missouri Baptist churches adopted the "Missouri Plan" which divided church offerings between the mission organizations of the two national conventions. This plan originated in the Third Baptist Church of St. Louis during the 1880s under the leadership of their pastor, John Priest Greene.

In 1919, the state convention considered and approved single alignment status with the Southern Baptist Convention. Individual churches were allowed to maintain a dual alignment with both conventions and several chose to do so. The president of William Jewell encouraged a policy of dual alignment for the college. That president was John Priest Greene.

Today, the college retains its formal denominational affiliations with American Baptist Churches, USA (formerly the Northern Baptist Convention), and the Missouri Baptist Convention. It is the only Baptist college in the country to be so aligned. The

College seal in stained glass at Gano Chapel

Dr. John Priest Greene in his college office about 1899. He served as president of William Jewell for thirty years.

college works very hard to maintain and strengthen its historic ties to both organizations. The college receives modest but growing financial support from individual ABC churches, and substantial financial support (approximately $1 million annually) from the Missouri Baptist Convention.

Throughout history, Jewell's expression of church heritage has been molded and strengthened by a succession of presidents, faculty, trustees, alumni, and students.

PRESIDENTS

William Jewell College has indeed made the presidency of the college a primary symbol of Christian heritage. While lay leaders could be as committed and as effective in maintaining this heritage, the board of trustees has consistently elected ordained ministers as presidents.

Fortunately, these ministers have contributed much more than "symbolism" to the college's Christian development. Several brought to the office of president a record of distinguished leadership as pastors of highly regarded churches-John Priest Greene from Third Baptist Church, St. Louis, Mo; John F. Herget from Ninth Street Baptist Church, Cincinnati, Ohio; Walter Pope Binns from First Baptist Church, Roanoke, Va; H. Guy Moore from Broadway Baptist Church, Ft. Worth, Texas; and Thomas S. Field from First Baptist Church, Springfield, Mo.

The presidents have also brought impressive leadership credentials from prior denominational work within state and national Baptist circles and other Protestant organizations. Between 1890 and 1908, John Priest Greene had received honorary degrees for church leadership from William Jewell College, Colgate University, Wake Forest College and Washington University. Walter Pope Binns was a prominent member and leader of national Protestant organizations including Americans United, which addressed church-state issues. Before becoming president of William Jewell, Thomas Field had been president of the board of trustees of Southwest Baptist College (now University). He also served two years as president of the Missouri Baptist Convention.

Gordon Kingsley provided service to the Missouri Baptist Convention by writing its sesqui-centennial history in 1984, *Frontiers: The Story of Missouri Baptists.* W. Christian Sizemore came to William Jewell from the presidency of Alderson-Broaddus College in Phillipi, W. Va., where he provided leadership to numerous projects and causes associated with the American Baptist Churches, USA.

All William Jewell presidents have demonstrated

a high regard for Christian education. This has resulted in a strong emphasis on academic quality, while remaining, in the words of the college mission statement, "loyal to the ideals of Christ and demonstrating a Christian philosophy for the whole of life."

FACULTY

Alumni can attest to the spiritual enrichment provided by college instructors. Study of the Bible and religion courses have always been a required part of the curriculum.

Hubert Inman Hester is a superb example of Christian commitment in the faculty ranks. During his fifty-seven-year association with the college, he served as professor of Bible, head of the Bible department, financial aid officer, vice president and interim president. He wrote twenty-three books. *The Heart of the Hebrew History* and *The Heart of the New Testament* sold millions of copies and were used as college textbooks throughout the United States and around the world. Hester was revered by students and faculty alike, who regularly filled his classroom to overflowing for an annual lecture on the crucifixion and the resurrection.

His commitment to the college and its students was evidenced during the Depression and war years by large numbers of students who often found themselves in financial difficulty. Dr. Hester would somehow find extra money for their tuition-often through the quiet contributions of his friends and acquaintances in area churches. Upon his death in 1983, he was eulogized by J. Gordon Kingsley with these words, "Hubert Inman Hester was a sage, a statesman, a saint. He was an eagle in dove's clothing, a giant who masqueraded as a leprechaun, a great man who eschewed the trappings of greatness. He was 'Doc,' the one, the only, the original, himself."

Another example of a devoted Christian teacher is David O. Moore. He came to the college in 1956 as professor of Bible and retired as chairman of the religion department in 1986. A significant controversy surrounded Dr. Moore in the late 1970s, involving his efforts to maintain academic freedom in the presentation of various theological interpretations. Baptists from around the state and the administration of the college supported him in this matter. Dr. Moore is fondly remembered by former students as a teacher who challenged students to think and develop their own personal theological views.

Tom Bray '49 came to the college in 1957 as the first full-time director of religious activities. This was a relatively new venture on college campuses around the nation. The program was initiated to provide career information and opportunities for students preparing for the ministry. The initial focus of the program was to send students to lead church revivals. Jewell continues to send both indi-

Hubert Inman Hester is remembered for his unusually long tenure at William Jewell and his accomplishments as a teacher, administrator, author, and counselor.

Ministry students gather in the library for their annual picture.

Ministry students Jason Moore and Matt Jackson lead a weekend project in a local church.

Students paint a water tank black to help warm the water during a service project in Guadalajara, Mexico.

vidual students and student teams to provide service to churches as a form of career preparation.

Jerry Cain came to William Jewell in 1978 as director of student ministries. He directed student programming and coordinated weekly chapel. Cain's positions were elevated during his tenure, first to college chaplain and later to collegiate vice president. In 1992 the college awarded him a doctor of sacred theology degree (*honoris causa*). Cain had a tremendous impact upon students in spiritual matters, particularly those involving ministerial career decisions and preparation. He became the college's de facto ambassador-of-good-will to churches throughout the region. He has spoken in nearly every Baptist church in Missouri, led youth retreats and youth camps. He was instrumental in the formation of William Jewell's Service Learning Program, placing students in hands-on service and mission experiences.

Upon his resignation in 1998 to become president of Judson College in Elgin, Ill., the college announced its intention to establish the *Jerry Cain Endowed Chaplaincy*. This endowment will provide perpetual support for the work of the college chaplain and for other religious activities.

Each of these individual faculty members, along with others who have served as religion professors, deans of the chapel and campus ministers, has promoted one of Jewell's most important early purposes: career preparation for ministry and service.

The Christian heritage of the college is in no way limited to faculty and staff members responsible for religious study and programming. Alumni of all generations can point to the high percentage of faculty who have provided strong examples of Christian service, both on the campus and in the community. Since the founding of the college, students have worshipped in Liberty churches alongside faculty, and been inspired by the faculty model of spiritual commitment.

TRUSTEES

Many trustees have contributed to Christian heritage through individual service to the college, their churches and in religious affairs. John B. Wornall was an active member of the Westport Baptist Church (now First Calvary) in Kansas City. He served two years as moderator of the Missouri Baptist General Association (now the Missouri Baptist Convention) and eleven years as moderator of the Blue River Baptist Association. When he died in 1892, he had served twenty-five years as the president of the Jewell board of trustees.

The Honorable Charles Hardin, brother-in-law

of Dr. William Jewell, served twenty years as a trustee until his death in 1892. He was a dedicated member of his church and a moderator of the Missouri Baptist General Association. In 1875, while a trustee, he was elected governor of Missouri.

Another early trustee of note was Rev. Xerxes X. Buckner. He served as pastor in Columbia and Boonville and later of the Second Baptist Church in Liberty. In 1867 he was elected to the board as its president. The years following the Civil War proved to be a difficult financial period for the college. As financial agent, he was effective in the creation of endowment funds and made significant financial contributions himself.

Lewis Bell Ely was also appointed to the board in 1867 and served as financial agent from 1877 until his election as president of the board in 1892. For twenty-five years he was Sunday School superintendent of First Baptist Church, Carrollton, Mo. His fund-raising efforts resulted in Jewell's first dormitory in 1880, which was named in his honor. He was so highly regarded that after his death in 1897 another dormitory (built in 1911) was named after him. This one was called "New Ely" and is the current Ely Hall on campus.

There are well-known examples of modern-day trustees who have been devoted lay leaders in their churches and denomination. These include William F. Yates '98 and Charles F. Curry. Yates served on the board from 1943 until his death in 1979. He was a life-long member and benefactor of the First

Baptist Church, Richmond, Mo. Curry was a distinguished member of the board who served for an extended period as president. He was a trustee of Baptist Memorial Hospital and a loyal member of Calvary (now First Calvary) Baptist Church, Kansas City, Mo.

Service learning students assist with Luis Palau Crusade in Kansas City.

A good representation of current board members have served as an officer of the state and national Baptist conventions. Currently, eight members of the Board are church pastors, while others on the board serve in leadership roles at many levels, ranging from the local church to state and national denominational work.

ALUMNI

Through the decades, William Jewell has had an excellent record of turning out successful pastors, college and seminary professors, lay church leaders, missionaries, chaplains and denominational leaders.

The Citation for Achievement provides ample evidence of this success. Citation recipients have included: Harold Sanders '32, former executive director of the Kentucky Baptist Convention; Ruth Everley Hayes '43; former missionary to China;

Through the 1960s, 70s and 80s the Confronters represented Christian Student Ministries and William Jewell throughout the midwest.

Vernon Elmore '43, former pastor of the First Baptist Church, Corpus Christi; Millard Berquist '32, former president of Midwestern Baptist Theological Seminary; Claude Rhea '50, former president of Palm Beach Atlantic College; Fred Young '47, retired dean of Central Baptist Theological Seminary and renowned Dead Sea Scrolls scholar; Harlan Spurgeon '53, executive of the Home Mission Board and Cooperative Baptist Fellowship; Paul Eppinger '55, executive director of the Arizona Ecumenical Council; David Keith '71, professor of music at Southwestern Baptist Theological Seminary; and Shirley Williams '60, director of the collegiate ministries department of the Missouri Baptist Convention.

Many other alumni have served or are currently serving in administrative or executive denominational positions. Two serve as executive directors of Baptist state conventions: Dr. David T. Bunch '53 is executive director/treasurer of the Colorado Baptist General Convention and Dr. Jim Earl Harding '69 serves as executive director of the Utah-Idaho Southern Baptist Convention. Two others serve as state convention directors of student ministries: Loy Reed '70 in Florida, and Ben Early

'66 in Wyoming. Tom Clifton '64 serves as president of Central Baptist Theological Seminary. Lee Porter '53 served for an extended period of time as recording secretary of the Southern Baptist Convention. Wally Buckner '75 has served as assistant vice president with the Home Mission Board of the Southern Baptist Convention, and Martha Barr '60 has served as the executive director of American Baptist Women.

STUDENTS

According to early student records, the college was serving ministerial students from its very beginning. Historical records indicate that in 1870-71 there were 152 students and forty-six were students preparing for ministry. In 1872-73 there were 109 students and fifty-four were ministerial. There were 250 students in 1891-92 and ninety-three were in the then-existing school of theology. According to the report for 1924, there were 420 students and sixty were ministerial students.

Missouri Baptists established a Board of Ministerial Education in 1858 to assist ministerial students at William Jewell College and collected money for a number of years to assist them. While the group had in mind the building of a dormitory for ministerial students, funds were insufficient for that venture. However, in 1873 a Ministerial Student's Boarding Club was established, which was instrumental in keeping a large number of young prospective ministers in the college. Currently the college provides two types of ministerial scholarships each year: scholarships for students pursuing Christian-related vocations and H.I. Hester ministerial scholarships.

In 1857, Missouri Baptists agreed to establish a school of theology at William Jewell College and by 1869 had raised $40,000 as an endowment. A special board of visitors was appointed to give general oversight. The school was named the Jeremiah Vardeman School of Theology (named after the first moderator of the Missouri Baptist General Association and a trustee of the college). President Thomas Rambaut served as its first professor with three other professors teaching in the school. In *Jewell Is Her Name,* H.I. Hester observed that "the school of theology was never intended to take the place of graduate-level training given to college graduates in a theological seminary." However, few ministerial students at the time had the opportunity to attend a seminary. The school also served non-ministerial students who wanted to take religion courses.

Early on in college history, students formed a Baptist Evangelical Society. Later a Ministerial Association served religious vocational students. Today's counterpart organization is called Sigma Epsilon Pi. There were sixty-two Christian vocation students in the fall of 1997.

INFLUENCING STUDENTS FOR CHRISTIAN LEADERSHIP AND LIFE

Dr. H.I. Hester once wrote, "It may be said with complete honesty that at William Jewell it has been the purpose of the faculty to minister to the students." While this has been obvious in religion classes, professors in other courses have also integrated faith and knowledge. The faculty, through their teaching, counsel and relationships, have always had a fundamental role in ministering to all students.

The Christian heritage of the college was manifest early on, and is evident in the rules outlined in Jewell's very first catalog (dated 1850-51). Rule number 7 reads:

A 1979 Christian Student Union group heads for Glorieta, New Mexico.

Students are required to attend punctually morning and evening prayers in college, and conduct themselves with decorum; and also to attend public worship, at some church, every Sabbath, in the forenoon-the church to be selected by themselves-and report on Monday. And their attendance at any church shall be considered a failure if they enter the church after the services have begun, or leave before they close.

CENTER OF SPIRITUAL LIFE

Since 1926, the John Gano Memorial Chapel has stood as an architectural symbol of Christian heritage. Minor renovations have taken place in the chapel in recent years and another renovation will be part of the sesquicentennial capital campaign. The addition of a bell and clock tower on the southeast corner of the building will be named to honor the service of President Walter Pope Binns. The auditorium of the chapel will be named the Thomas and Virginia Field Convocation and Worship Center. A new pipe organ will be an added feature. A small addition to the side of the chapel will house the William E. Partee Center for Baptist Historical Studies and provide "green room" space for performers and program participants.

Chapel services in Gano have been a vital part of student life ever since the chapel was built. Faculty, administrators, area clergy, special visitors and students have all taken turns leading these services. Before the building of Gano, chapel services were held in Marston Hall (1915-1926), Wornall Hall (1896-1913) and Jewell Hall (1850-1896). In Jewell's early days, chapel services were held four days a week and attendance was required. During the days of compulsory chapel, students were assigned to seats in alphabetical order while faculty members took roll in assigned sections. While many students did not want to attend chapel at the time, and devised creative ways to miss and still be counted in attendance, these alumni now look back upon chapel as a meaningful time which fostered community bonding. Chapel services are now held one morning per week, with attendance voluntary. Attendance averages about 300-to-400 weekly, out of a student body of approximately 1,200. Chapel is in fact the most highly attended campus event outside football games.

Recently, the Grand River Baptist Church, Jameson, Mo., disbanded and donated its building to William Jewell College. In 1992, the college moved the building to campus as a visible reminder of the important role of small rural churches in feeding prospective students to Jewell. The chapel is used for small religious services, as well as many weddings. Beautifully restored and handsomely appointed with period furnishings and new stained glass, the chapel is open twenty-four hours a day for student prayer and meditation.

STUDENT PROGRAMMING

During 1946-47 interest developed in the work of the Baptist Student Union, sponsored by the Southern Baptist Convention. As a result, the college began holding a Religious Focus Week each year. A special speaker conducted the chapel services and spoke in classes. Special seminars were held in the evenings. Now, the college sponsors a similar program, "Christian Celebration Week." Christian Student Ministries (CSM) serves the students in place of the Baptist Student Union. The CSM Servant Council is an umbrella organization made up of students who help coordinate the various student religious programs. Often students involved in CSM serve as summer missionaries.

The Shepherd Program meets the spiritual needs of students by placing a student as a peer "chaplain" on floors of residence halls. These students attend a retreat for training in pastoral skills, evangelism and Bible study leadership. Also, student groups such as "Greek Council for Christ" serve in fraternities and sororities. Alpha Omega is a Christian sorority that provides spiritual discipling for William Jewell College women. "Freshman Share Group" provides nurture and care for freshman students.

HERITAGE IN THE CHRISTIAN COMMUNITY

William Jewell has always had a strong influence on Christian activities in surrounding communities. For example, during its early days the college maintained a branch of the Young Men's Christian Association.

The tradition of community service continues today with "Serve and Celebrate Day." Prior to Homecoming, students and faculty do service projects in the community. During a recent "Serve and Celebrate Day," 200 students participated in sixteen community projects.

Other examples of service include sport camps for inner-city youth, sponsored by the Fellowship of Christian Athletes, and the active homebuilding ministry of Habitat for Humanity, one of the first college-affiliated chapters in the country.

In 1982, the college began a Christmas tradition in downtown Kansas City. "The City Come Again" takes place at Grace and Holy Trinity Cathedral. The program, offering holiday choral and handbell music and a homily by the president, is offered annually as William Jewell's Christmas gift to Kansas City.

Executive council of B.S.U. in 1955. From left, seated— Diane Adams, Joy Bergman, Paul Eppinger, Bill Jackson, Betsy Morgan, Lila Wyss. Standing— Mary Ann Nance, Carolyn White, Fred Pryor, Ron Richmond, Lois Jacobson.

25

Each year students participate in "service learning." They take classes and then do an overseas mission trip. Students have been to Haiti, the Dominican Republic, Mexico, Brazil, Guatemala, Nicaragua, Mali and Jamaica. Other service opportunities occur closer to home, with students ministering to the needs of inner city residents in Kansas City.

HERITAGE IN THE BAPTIST COMMUNITY

Dr. H.I. Hester observed, "William Jewell has always been a denominational college," and so the college has always participated in the life of the Baptist community.

Second Baptist Church of Liberty has always been a sister institution to William Jewell. Within a year of founding, Jewell rented the basement of the church to conduct classes. In return, the president and other faculty members provided full-time preaching at the church, an uncommon occurrence in the mid-nineteenth century. The college continues its relationship with the church as many administrators, faculty members, students, and trustees attend services there. Since the founding of the college, the church has provided its sanctuary for the annual spring baccalaureate service.

William Jewell College also extended its hand to sister Baptist institutions in Missouri. Southwest Baptist College (now University), Bolivar, Mo., and Grand River College, Gallatin, Mo., were not able to continue operation during the early part of the twentieth century because of financial difficulties. William Jewell operated both of these institutions for awhile. Southwest Baptist College finally was able to secure adequate finances to resume independent operation but Grand River College succumbed.

The Missouri Baptist Historical Society began in 1885 through the efforts of a William Jewell faculty member, James R. Eaton, and others. As the Society collected articles that needed an archive, the William Jewell library provided space. In 1962 the Missouri Baptist Convention created an historical commission and voted that its archives be permanently housed at William Jewell. As caretaker of the archives, the college entered into an agreement with the Missouri Baptist Convention in 1981 to create and support a center for Baptist historical studies in the midwest.

The center's first director was Dr. Adrian Lamkin, who left the college in 1997. In 1985, the center was endowed with a major gift from William E. Partee '25, an attorney from Hannibal, Mo., who died in August 1998. Today, Dr. Donald V. Wideman is executive director while Angela Stiffler '90 serves as the archivist of the William E. Partee Center for Baptist Historical Studies.

William Jewell College purchased the library of the famed London preacher, Charles Haddon Spurgeon, in 1905. It included 6,618 volumes.

When the college officially opened the Charles F. Curry Library in 1965, a special room replicating Spurgeon's study was created to house his collection. It has been the focus of many researchers of Spurgeon and Puritan Christianity.

When John Priest Greene was a student in Germany, he began to copy by hand the works of the Anabaptist Balthasar Hubmaier. Unfortunately, these notes were lost when Wornall Hall burned in 1913. However, Dr. Greene was determined to obtain copies of Hubmaier's works. Later he was able to get photographic copies of all of Hubmaier's extant works. Dr. George Davidson, a William Jewell professor, translated them. Both the photographic copies and the translations are housed in the Jewelliana collection of the college library. This is one of America's finest links with Baptists' Anabaptist heritage.

A more recent role in the life of the Baptist community has been established by church-college consultants. Dr. Field developed the idea during his presidency so that the college could strengthen its relationship with Missouri Baptist churches. Dr. Loren Goings '32 was the first person in this position and continues in this role today. Today, there are many consultants who represent the college at a wide variety of Baptist-related meetings, conventions, retreats and other functions. The consultants are often retired ministers and lay leaders who have provided distinguished service to the denomination.

SUMMARY

Everyone associated with William Jewell knows that Christian heritage has been fundamental to the history and life of the institution. Since the presidency of John Priest Greene the college community has been able to point to this heritage through the college motto, *Deo Fisus Labora*—Trust in God, and Work. The motto is displayed in college seals around campus, in the stained glass windows of Gano Chapel, and now on the William Jewell collegiate license plate in Missouri. It serves as a reminder of educational heritage and the collegiate philosophy that faith and work are vital in life. Generations of alumni can attest that the William Jewell experience provides quality preparation—both spiritually and academically—to be contributing members of the local and global community. *Deo Fisus Labora!*

Charles Haddon Spurgeon

CAMPUS BUILDINGS

High Upon a Hill She Stands

by Jerry Cain

*I*n the September 1996 edition of *Atlantic Monthly*, James Howard Kunstler made the following observation:

"The buildings our predecessors constructed paid homage to history in their design, including elegant solutions to age old problems posed by the cycles of weather and light, and they paid respect to the future in the sheer expectation that they would endure through the lifetimes of the people who built them. They therefore embodied a sense of chronological connectivity, which lends meaning and dignity to our little lives. It puts us in touch with the ages and with the eternities, suggesting that we are part of a larger and more significant organism. It even suggests that the larger organism we are part of cares about us and puts us in touch with the holy."

If Kunstler is correct, the buildings at William

Jewell College are a holy history of who we are, where we came from and where we are going. Thus, this recitation of the structures now seen on campus will embody more than a listing of names, dates, places, square footages, and construction costs. It will be a story of the people who studied, taught, led, dreamed, and gave their lives and fortunes to those yet coming to the Hill.

JEWELL HALL (1852)

As the Parthenon crowns the Acropolis of ancient Athens, Jewell Hall crowns the highest hill in Clay County as the oldest building and centerpiece facility of William Jewell College. This outstanding example of classic Greek revival architecture was begun in 1850, occupied in 1852, but not completed until 1858. Jewell Hall originally housed

the entire college including offices, classrooms, residence hall, library and societies. Twice during the Civil War it also served as quarters for Union soldiers in the area.

The building is named for Dr. William Jewell, the namesake of the college and one of the most influential persons in Missouri life during the first thirty years of statehood. Born on New Year's Day 1789 in Virginia, he moved with his family to Kentucky where he studied medicine at Transylvania University, which was founded in 1780 by John Gano, the namesake of the chapel at William Jewell College. Jewell eventually came to Missouri in 1821, the year of statehood, and set up a medical practice in Columbia. He was known as a good physician who expected integrity and quality from his peers and payment from his patients. As a civic leader, Jewell was instrumental in the founding of Columbia, Mo. He also served in the state legislature where he fought for the abolition of the whipping post and pillory and used his influence to help establish Columbia College, which later became the University of Missouri. He emancipated some of his slaves in 1836, but did not free all of them until his death.

As a religious leader, Jewell served as a member of the Little Bonne Femme Baptist Church. He was also one of the founders of the First Baptist Church of Columbia where a Sunday School class still bears his name. Jewell offered the Missouri Baptist General Association $10,000 to begin their

first college, which they accepted, receiving the charter for the college on February 27, 1849.

On August 21, 1849, representatives of six communities arrived in Boonville to submit proposals for the location of the new educational enterprise. The bid from Liberty, extended by Col. Alexander Doniphan, was accepted over proposals from Palmyra, Boonville, and Fulton. To ensure the gift of Dr. Jewell, who had originally supported the Boonville location for the college, Doniphan suggested the school be named William Jewell College in honor of its first benefactor and founding philanthropist.

Jewell literally gave his life superintending the construction of the building that bears his name. He expected good workmanship from his contractors and on one occasion required them to tear down a 15' x 60' section of wall because it was not built on a good foundation. On August 6, 1852, Jewell suffered a heat stroke while working on the building and died a day later. Last refurbished in 1949 during the centennial of William Jewell College, Jewell Hall now serves as a classroom facility and houses offices of the departments of language, business, and English.

THE PRESIDENT'S HOME (1905)

In 1892 Dr. John Priest Greene left his pastorate at the Third Baptist Church in St. Louis to become president of William Jewell College. When

Mr. A.D. Brown, owner of Brown Shoe Company in St. Louis, visited his former pastor in Liberty, he was distressed to see what he considered inadequate housing for Greene and his family. Subsequently, Brown donated $25,000 to the college for the building of a spacious, beautiful home for the president, which would also serve as a gathering place and social center for the campus. The trustees pledged an additional $15,000 to furnish the home and construction began in 1904.

Since it was opened in 1905, eight college presidents have lived in this home, though they have not been the sole occupants. During World War II (1942-44), the house was used as a dormitory for women so the Navy cadets in school on the campus could occupy the women's residence halls. Later, from 1946 to 1948, the house was used for classrooms and faculty offices while Jewell Hall was being renovated for the college's centennial. In 1949 the house was reconditioned to become again the home of the president.

The President's Home is constructed in a modified Georgian style of red brick with white columns on the south portico and a porte cochere on the east side of the building. In 1995 the house underwent massive reconstruction as it was replumbed, reroofed, rewired, repaired, and repainted. Bathrooms and the kitchen were updated, the original floors uncovered and refinished, and a forced-air heating and air conditioning system was installed to replace the hot water heating system. President W. Christian Sizemore and First Lady Anne Sizemore serve as gracious hosts to thousands of students, teachers, alumni, trustees, and visitors who frequent the President's Home annually.

THE LEGACY OF LEWIS B. ELY (1880, 1911)

At age thirteen, Lewis B. Ely moved with his family from Frankfort, Ky. (where John Gano is buried), to Missouri, beginning his long connection with the First Baptist Church of Carrollton and eventually with William Jewell College. As merchant and businessman, he began working for Captain William Hill at Hill's Landing on the Missouri River, purchasing the business in 1862 when the owner died. Ely served as a trustee of William Jewell College from 1867 until 1897 and as chairman of the board from 1892 until his death five years later. Formally retiring from business in 1875, Ely dedicated the rest of his life to William Jewell College as a financial agent.

The President's Home, 1905

New Ely Hall, 1911

Ely had a great love for children and considered his work at William Jewell College only an extension of his Sunday School work in Carrollton, where he was superintendent for twenty-five years at First Baptist Church. He provided leadership in Christian education societies, served three terms as moderator of the Missouri Baptist General Association (now Missouri Baptist Convention), and was elected vice president of the Southern Baptist Convention.

In twenty years of service to the college, Ely quadrupled the endowment from $50,000 to over $200,000. He raised $40,000 to build Wornall Hall (1896) and $11,000 for the first residence hall on campus, the one that would bear his name, Ely Hall. Built in 1880, the building was initially used

as a dormitory for men and a dining hall for the entire college. It was constructed approximately fifty feet north of Jewell Hall where the present flagpole stands. In 1910 the original Ely Hall became known as Old Ely because a new $100,000 building was constructed. The new fireproof Ely Hall, the first of its kind in Missouri, was constructed as additional residential space and occupied by men in the fall of 1911. Old Ely continued to serve as a residence hall, dining hall, and college union until 1958 when it was torn down and its functions were assumed by the new Yates College Union and Browning Hall.

New Ely Hall, fully air-conditioned and reconditioned in 1995, now houses first-year and sophomore women in its top three floors while the base-

Marston Hall, 1914

ment serves as the offices for facilities management, housekeeping, security, and the college infirmary.

MISSIONARY MEMORIALIZED IN MARSTON HALL (1914)

Marston Hall was built in 1914 as a quick response to the fire that destroyed Wornall Hall, the first science building on campus, in August of 1913. All of the scientific equipment of the college, as well as many long-term research projects, were destroyed in the Wornall Hall disaster. Though Marston Hall was begun promptly, the bankruptcy of the contractor caused the building effort to cease before the project was completed. Desperate professors and eager students installed the plumbing and wiring themselves in an attempt to make the shell usable for classroom facilities. The chemistry and physics departments moved into the building before it was finished. Marston Hall was remodeled and upgraded in 1953 and again in 1993 when the sciences moved to the new White Science Center to be replaced by the departments of nursing education, political science, history, the Fine Arts Program, and the advancement team of the college.

The building was named for Dr. Sylvester W. Marston, a native of Maine who moved to Missouri to begin his ministry in 1865. After serving as president of the Boonville Institute for three years, Marston spent the next five years in Christian education across the state increasing the number of Sunday Schools. In 1873 he became superintendent of state missions for Missouri Baptists, leaving that position in 1876 to accept an appointment from President Ulysses S. Grant to become United States Agent for the civilized tribes of the Indian Territory. His final ministry role was with the American Baptist Home Mission Society where he served as superintendent of Freedmen's Missions. President John Priest Greene persuaded his friend Edgar L. Marston, a prominent New York businessman and son of Sylvester Marston, to provide the funds for the building in honor of his father.

MELROSE HALL (1925)

The headline in the September 25, 1917, *Student* announced a new experiment in education at William Jewell College, "Girls, Girls and Girls." On December 9, 1920, the trustees voted to admit women on the same terms as men, thus creating the need for women's housing and Melrose Hall. Mr. C.M. Treat of Pasadena, Calif., offered $50,000 to the college for the construction of Melrose Hall on the condition that a chapel and gymnasium be built also. The trustees accepted his offer and by January 1, 1925, announced that funds had been secured for all three structures.

The modern, four-story residence hall was placed on the northwest corner of the campus, north of the President's Home. Named Melrose Hall at the request of Treat, it was occupied in the fall of 1926. The stately residence hall, completely air-conditioned and renovated in 1994, serves as home to first-year women at William Jewell College.

Melrose Hall, 1925

JOHN GANO MEMORIAL CHAPEL (1926)

John Gano, a descendent of French Huguenots tracing a lineage back through Etienne Gayneau, was born in New Jersey in 1727. Though his father, Daniel Gano, was a Presbyterian, he gave his son permission to join the Baptist Church in Hopewell, N.J., the church of his mother. Gano was an early missionary in the South, where he made evangelistic tours to Virginia and the Carolinas on behalf of the Philadelphia Association. He was ordained in May of 1754 and became pastor for the Baptist Church in Morristown, N.J., and later for the Baptist Church in Yadkin, N.C. In 1762 he became pastor of the First Baptist Church of New York where he ministered for twenty-six years.

During the war for independence, he joined the Continental Army and served as a chaplain for

Gen. James Clinton and Gen. George Washington. At the war's end, Washington asked Gano to lead the troops in prayer during the cessation of hostilities. There is also questionable, though significant evidence that Gano immersed Washington for an adult baptism during the war.

John Gano Memorial Chapel, 1926

At the conclusion of the war, Gano moved to Frankfort, Ky., where he was elected chaplain of the Kentucky Senate and was ultimately buried with his wife, Sarah. Always an advocate of education, Gano was one of the founders of Rhode Island College (now Brown University) and served as a trustee of Columbia University in New York. While in Frankfort, he helped to establish

Transylvania University in Lexington (in 1780), the college from which a young medical student named William Jewell would graduate in 1820.

In 1924 William Jewell College President Harry Wayman announced the imminent construction of a new chapel where Wornall Hall had previously stood. In the fall of 1925, excavation began for the new building which would serve as the school's central assembly hall.

Upon completion on November 22, 1925, the 112' x 67' building had a seating capacity of 1,100 and housed administrative offices such as the college president, dean, registrar, cashier, and secretary on the balcony level. There was also room for two assembly rooms for literary societies and a basement that would serve numerous purposes over the next seventy years. In connection

New Brown Gymnasium, 1929

with the laying of the cornerstone, it was announced that Elizabeth Price Johnson of Kansas City had given a significant donation to the chapel in honor of her great grandfather, Rev. John Gano. Thus, on September 26, 1926, John Gano Memorial Chapel was dedicated. The chapel was the founding venue of the William Jewell College Fine Arts Program and remains the worship center of the campus. In

the last seventy-five years, the building has housed the William Jewell Press, the music department, the campus snack bar, drama department, electrical shop, student ministries, the New Horizons lounge and religion department offices. The balcony offices were renovated in 1986 through a gift from the Allen J. Neth family to hold offices for the religion department, campus ministries, and chaplain. Six years later, the front of the stage was rebuilt and new seating was placed in the auditorium section, reducing the capacity of the John Gano Memorial Chapel to just over 800.

THE BROWN GYMNASIUMS AND BROWN HALL (1893, 1929)

Though he served as a trustee only from 1909 until his death in 1913, Mr. Alanson D. Brown played a significant role in the development of William Jewell College. He was the power behind the President's Home and the first gymnasium at the college. In the 1870s Brown became founding partner and president of Hamilton-Brown Shoe Company. He started the firm without any outside capital and helped it grow to be one of the largest shoe companies in the world. Brown was a member of the Third Baptist Church in St. Louis, where he was befriended by longtime pastor John Priest Greene. Brown and Greene toured Europe together in the summer of 1912, one year before Brown died of leukemia in San Antonio, Texas.

The first Brown Gymnasium, 40' x 100', was constructed in 1896 for $12,300 with a basement, main floor, and gallery level. Located at the site of the present faculty parking lot, it was deemed as the "best, most complete facility west of the Mississippi." Brown Gymnasium was the first building at the college to be used solely as a gymnasium and was lighted by electricity and ventilated by 240 windows. The original running gallery around the inside of the facility had to be removed about 1900 when basketball became a popular sport, and by 1925 the basketball crowds had outgrown Brown Gymnasium so that games were being played at Liberty High School. Brown Gymnasium mysteriously burned to the ground on January 30, 1928, with sparks from the fire threatening venerable Jewell Hall.

With the combination of approximately $10,000 the students had raised and $26,000 from the insurance company, there was enough capital to begin the construction of the New Brown Gymnasium in April of 1928. J.P. Reynolds, president of Kansas City Life Insurance Company, and W.D. Johnson, vice president of Fidelity Trust Company, subscribed $20,000 to rebuild the structure. Finished in December of 1928, the new building was a three-story structure, 101' x 155', including three basketball courts and a balcony with total seating of 1,300. A swimming pool-which had been excluded from the first gymnasium-was included in the basement level of the new Brown Gym. The third floor served as handball courts, classroom space, and a faculty locker room and gym.

The new Brown Gymnasium was dedicated on Thursday, January 2, 1930, with the formal address delivered by Lt. Gov. Edward J. Winter. After additional preliminary remarks, the first basketball game in the new building was played between the William Jewell Cardinals and the University of Missouri Tigers, the Cardinals losing 22-38.

With the construction of the Mabee Center for Physical Education in 1980, Brown Gymnasium underwent a renovation in 1983 and was renamed Brown Hall. Dr. Harvey Thomas, trustee, was director of the Brown renovation campaign, which helped raise the $3,500,000 necessary to accomplish the task. Part of the new renovation included Peters Theater, named for alum and insurance agent Garnett M. Peters whose monetary gift made the theater possible. Its opening performance in October of 1983 was a special recognition of Virginia D. Rice, longtime professor of communication and drama at the college. The Brown Hall renovation was completed in the early spring of 1984 and now houses the radio station (KWJC), student newspaper (*Hilltop Monitor*), communication department, art department, psychology department as well as the admission offices. The third floor of the building which formerly had handball courts and classrooms, now contains the Ruth E. Stocksdale Gallery of Art. A conference room named for the Mexican War hero, Liberty resident, and co-founder of William Jewell College, Alexander Doniphan, occupies the southwest corner of the third floor. This building also includes the Evening Division office complex. To the south of the entrance is a courtyard dedicated to the memory of Bruce Thomson, formerly a professor of sociology, dean, and executive vice president of the college.

JOHN PRIEST GREENE MEMORIAL HALL (1949)

Completed in the centennial year of the college, 1949, the administration building honors the leadership of John Priest Greene, president of the college from 1892 to 1920 and from 1921 to 1923.

John Priest Greene Memorial Hall, 1949

Greene was a native Missourian, born in 1849 and educated at Memphis Academy, LaGrange College, Southern Baptist Seminary, and the University of Leipzig. He pastored in Louisville, Ky., before coming to pastor the Third Baptist Church of St. Louis, which experienced phenomenal growth under his leadership from 1882 until he became president of the college in 1892.

W.D. Johnson, also honored in Greene Hall, had moved to Kansas City from Texas near the turn of the century. He served as a trustee from 1909 until 1949 and was elected chairman each year from 1925 until 1949. Johnson was a member of the (First) Calvary Baptist Church in Kansas City and spent his life as a farmer, merchant, banker, insurance executive, rancher, and cattleman. During his tenure on the board, he worked with five college presidents. Because he was a man of quiet conviction and deep devotion, his gifts came to the college without public acclaim. During the Great Depression, Johnson would check with President Herget at the end of each month and make a gift large enough to pay whatever bills could not be paid through the regular income of the school. It is conservatively estimated that his total gifts amounted to at least $1.5 million before his death on April 13, 1951.

Under the leadership of President Walter Pope Binns, Johnson pledged a gift of $200,000 to build an administration building in honor of his friend, John Priest Greene. The advent of World War II prevented the construction and, thus, the building was not begun until after the war was over. Johnson pledged the gift at Commencement in 1942, the same year that he gave $250,000 to the college for the endowment of the department of religion and philosophy. Completed in 1949, the centennial of the college and the anniversary of Dr. Greene's birth, Greene Hall was dedicated on

December 1 in conjunction with the annual Achievement Day activities under Dr. Binns' leadership. Included on the program were Elizabeth Ann Johnson and Nancy Jane Green, both grandchildren of Johnson and President Greene. (By a strange coincidence, Mrs. Greene, the widow of Dr. Greene, passed away at their home in California the very hour the building was dedicated.)

The three stories of the facility are designed in colonial fashion and house the administrative offices of the president, provost and academic vice president, marketing and communications, overseas studies, registrar, student financial planning, business office and mail room.

JONES HALL (1954)

After World War II, the women's enrollment at William Jewell College increased as rapidly as the men's enrollment. Melrose Hall had served as the only residence hall for women since 1926, though three off-campus houses had been purchased to handle the residential needs of women during the war when the dormitories were occupied by the Navy School. A second women's residence hall, costing $121,000, was built to accommodate fifty-four women to meet the additional demands of increased enrollment. Occupied in 1954, the new residence hall was named for Minetry Jones, Jr., a 1914 graduate of William Jewell College. Jones served as trustee of the college from 1932 to 1938

Jones Hall, 1954

when he was appointed assistant to the president and later administrative vice president. In July of 1962 he served as interim president between the administrations of Walter Pope Binns and H. Guy Moore.

GREENE STADIUM AND PATTERSON FIELD (1955, 1992)

When football started at William Jewell College in 1888, there were only eleven players. One of those few was Luther D. Greene of Richmond, Mo., who served not only as halfback but also as manager of the team with responsibility for raising funds and running the team. He was present when Greene Stadium was dedicated on September 17, 1955, in his honor as William Jewell defeated Ottawa, 28-13. The ceremonies of the day included the living captains of all the Cardinal teams since 1888. Greene brought honor to William Jewell College through a career as a physician and state legislator from his hometown.

Completed in 1955 at a cost of $95,200, Greene Stadium boasts a concession stand, ticket windows, restrooms, press rooms, storage, and thirty-two rows of seats that can hold up to 5,000 football fans. In 1992 the football field inside Greene Stadium was named for legendary coach Norris Patterson. A native of Odessa, Mo., Patterson studied at Missouri Valley College before joining the coaching staff of William Jewell in 1950. In his eighteen years at Jewell the Cardinals had an overall record of 134-33-9, including thirteen championships and five second-place finishes. Patterson's honors also include being elected to the NAIA Football Hall of Fame, NACDA Athletic Directors Hall of Fame, Missouri Valley College Hall of Fame, and in 1989 the William Jewell Hall of Distinguished Teachers.

Semple Hall, 1957

SEMPLE HALL (1957)

Dedicated at Homecoming on November 9, 1957, along with Yates College Union, Semple Hall became the third women's residence. Located behind Melrose Hall (1926) and Jones Hall (1954), the building was named for Dr. Robert Baylor Semple who taught at the college for forty years, 1868-1908. Semple was born in Virginia in 1842 and converted under the ministry of Rev. John A. Broadus in 1859. The Rev. Dr. William F. Broaddus, an uncle by whom the orphaned Semple was reared, directed his early education. After graduating from the University of Virginia and serving in the Confederate Army, Semple came to William Jewell College in 1868. As head of the department of ancient languages, he had professional duties which included teaching Latin, German, Greek and Roman history. Students fondly remembered Semple's heroes as Socrates, the apostle Paul and Stonewall Jackson and thus nicknamed him "Old Soc." He served twice as president of the American Association of University Professors. After he died in 1909, Semple was buried in Fairview Cemetery in Liberty.

R.B. Semple's son, Dr. William T. Semple '00, was a distinguished businessman in Cincinnati who served as trustee at the college from 1937 until his death in 1962. From 1943 to 1949, he was a member of the Centennial Campaign Committee and endowed the departments of Latin and Greek with a gift of $250,000.

Begun in 1956, Semple Hall was finished a year later, at a cost of $436,000, and occupied by 121 women. A wing was added in 1966 to house an additional seventy women. The building currently houses the four sororities of the college as well as non-Greek students.

YATES COLLEGE UNION (1958)

Yates College Union, the first structure built on campus to specifically accommodate student activities, was dedicated on Homecoming Day on November 9, 1957, along with Semple Hall. The first section of Yates College Union was finished in 1958 at a cost of $500,000. The original structure included 25,000 square feet and provided space for the dining needs of 500 resident students and the extracurricular activities of an enrollment of 1,000. Previously, some extracurricular activities were located in the basement of Gano Chapel. The new air-conditioned structure encompassed a cafeteria, the bookstore, and conference rooms, offices for students and staff, and lockers and storage areas.

The building was named in honor of Mr. Will F. Yates, class of 1898, and prominent businessman and trustee of the college. Yates had given $250,000 to endow the department of chemistry in memory of his son, James Andrew Yates, who had graduated in 1927 with a chemistry major but died soon after graduation. Educated in a country

Yates College Union, 1958

school in Ray County, Will Yates arrived in Liberty in the fall of 1893 at age sixteen to begin his relationship with William Jewell College. Upon graduation he had hoped to spend his career teaching but could only find a job in a bank. In 1901 he was hired by the Exchange Bank of Richmond where he worked for seventy-one years and became chairman of the board of directors. Of the four banks in Richmond during the Depression, his Exchange Bank was the only one to survive. He was proud of not having to foreclose on Ray County and area farmers. In 1942 Yates joined the board of trustees at William Jewell College where he served until his death at age 101 in February of 1979.

In 1966 a new three-level wing of 21,285 square feet was adjoined to the existing building at

Eaton Hall, 1958

a cost of $900,000. The enlarged structure was to facilitate the activities of 1,500 students with a food service capacity of 1,200. The new addition also featured a second cafeteria, lounge, snack bar, and meeting rooms. The Union was expanded in anticipation of two major residence halls, Eaton and Browning, to be built in the future.

EATON HALL (1958)

As Yates College Union neared completion and Old Ely Hall continued to deteriorate, the trustees authorized a plan for a new campus residence hall in response to the ever-changing needs of the college and the continued growth of the student population. Thus, in the fall of 1958, 124 men moved into the newly completed and fully air-conditioned $461,000 Eaton Hall, the second campus facility to be named for a professor.

James R. Eaton taught natural science at the college from 1869 until 1896. He was the second son of George W. Eaton, president of Madison

(now Colgate) University in Hamilton, N.Y., from which he was awarded bachelor's, master's, and doctoral degrees. He was a member of Phi Beta Kappa Society and a fellow of the American Association for the Advancement of Science. His classroom motto was, "What is worth doing at all is worth doing well." Eaton was one of the first in America to combine the study of theology and science. A story in an 1881 edition of the *Student* says, "He is in full sympathy with the progress of science but does not place it above the Bible, believing, as he does, that true science and religion are in perfect accord with one another." In an attempt to regain his failing health, Eaton embarked on a tour of the Mediterranean only to die in Cairo, Egypt, in March of 1897, where he was buried.

His son, Hubert Eaton, served faithfully on the board of trustees from 1938 until 1958. The founder of Forest Lawn Mortuary and Gardens in Glendale, Calif., Hubert Eaton served on search committees for two presidents and helped fund the Balthasar Hubmaier Collection in Curry Library. He gave more than $200,000 to the college.

MARGUERITE APARTMENTS AT REGENT'S QUADRANGLE (1962)

In the 1950s, Ray Johnson, '13, was concerned that the married students at William Jewell College, unlike their single peers, were left to fend for themselves when it came to housing arrangements. Until the post-war years, this was not a major problem as small houses or basement apartments could be rented in Liberty for reasonable rates. However, the number of married students grew significantly in the 1950s creating a housing shortage for this segment of the student body.

Thus, construction began in 1961 on the north side of the campus facing Doniphan Street of three buildings with twelve apartments each. The two-story brick buildings were named in honor of Johnson's wife, Marguerite. One of the buildings was specifically reserved for the use of married ministerial students. On Sunday afternoon, October 21, 1962, the apartments were dedicated with the final cost tallied at $48,471. All of the apartments have two bedrooms with bathroom, kitchen and living room. Besides providing housing for married couples, some units are used by visiting scholars, the missionary in residence or even single students. In 1987 the parking areas around the Marguerite Apartments as well as the playground and other facilities were named Regent's Quadrangle in appreciation of Jewell's overseas ties with Regent's Park, the Baptist college of Oxford University.

LIBRARIES AT WILLIAM JEWELL COLLEGE (1908, 1965)

From the founding of the college in 1849 until 1908, the necessary books for a liberal arts educa-

tion were kept in several locations in Jewell Hall. The library staff varied throughout those years as did the rules outlining the use of materials in the library. In 1906 the purchase of the private library of London's Puritan preacher, Charles Haddon Spurgeon, necessitated the construction of the first library building at William Jewell College.

A gift of $30,000 from Andrew Carnegie was secured toward the construction of the $61,000 facility, which was finished in 1908. Named for Carnegie, the library contained over 17,000 vol-

Carnegie Library, 1908

Charles F. Curry Library, 1965

umes, which were moved by students from Jewell Hall to the new facility in less than half a day, that day being declared a holiday by the college administration. The movement to the new building was so carefully planned that not one of the volumes was lost and only a small number of books were out of

41

Browning Hall, 1967

place once the transfer was completed. In addition to the C.H. Spurgeon collection, the new Carnegie Library contained the Mertins' collection of autographs and holographs; the only complete collection of the writings of Anabaptist martyr Balthasar Hubmaier; the Ted Malone collection of poems used in his radio program "Between the Bookends;" and the federal government publications deposited with the library.

That building also proved inadequate and a new library facility was constructed in 1964 on the site of the original Carnegie Library. History repeated itself when more than 450 William Jewell students were provided a steak dinner to move the 87,000 volumes into the new four-story library with over 58,000 feet of floor space. New collections added to the facility included the Missouri Baptist Historical Collection, which details the history of Missouri Baptists, and the Jewell Heritage Collection, which chronicles the history of William Jewell College. The facility, costing $1,250,000, was opened in August of 1965.

In 1970 the trustees voted unanimously to name the building for Charles F. Curry, who served on the board of trustees from 1948 until 1968 and was chairman from 1954 to 1968. A member of (First) Calvary Baptist Church, Curry was a well-known real estate developer in Kansas City, contributing not only to William Jewell College but also to Baptist Memorial Hospital and Midwestern Seminary. When presenting him with a Distinguished Citizen Award in 1961, fellow Democrat Harry Truman said, "Charlie Curry is a great citizen of our community, who has helped many, including the one you're looking at."

THE LEGACY OF WILLIAM P. BROWNING (1967)

The son of a Missouri cattleman, William P. Browning was born in 1885 on a farm near Mexico, Mo., where he lived until age thirteen when his family moved to Kansas City. He graduated from Central High School where he studied Latin and Greek before coming to William Jewell College to major in modern languages. He was a member of the Sigma Nu fraternity and one of the founders of Aeons, a senior honorary for men. Browning was an avid tennis player, football fan, worked on the first *Tatler* yearbook, and occasionally submitted articles and artwork for the *Student*. In 1929 he joined William Jewell's board of trustees, serving as president from 1950-54 and vice president from 1962-66 before retiring from the board in 1977. In 1947, during the Centennial Campaign of the college, Browning gave the college 341 acres to the north side of the campus in memory of his parents. The contribution is still called "the Browning Campus," and was noted in 1964 when the theater on the ground floor of the Curry Library was named in his honor. This quiet and efficient man, a charter member of the Wornall Road Baptist Church in Kansas City, gave additional acreage to the college upon his death in 1977.

In 1967 a new four-level men's residence hall was constructed and named for Browning. This building of 28,620 square feet was to house 180 men and was completed at a cost of $800,000. With renovations in 1994, Browning Hall became the first residence hall to have single rooms reserved for upper-class students and the first residence hall to house both females and males, with men on the first three levels and women on the fourth floor.

PILLSBURY MUSIC CENTER (1974)

The music building had been a priority for the trustees and administration since 1961. In the fall of 1971 procedures were set in motion to construct the new building, but the official ground breaking was not until Founder's Day on March 6, 1973, also the 125th anniversary of the college.

The Pillsbury Music Center is a four-level

structure of Georgian style, originally opened on Homecoming Day, October 27, 1974, though not formally named until November 15, 1980, in honor of the Pillsbury Foundation and the prominent St. Louis family which has given generously to the college. Three generations of the Pillsbury family have served on the board of trustees at William Jewell College, including E.S. Pillsbury, Fred Pillsbury, and Linda Pillsbury Roos. The building, constructed at a cost of $1.4 million, includes a choral suite with a capacity of 120 and a recital hall that seats 125. The recital hall is named for Wes Forbis, former chairman of the department and national editor of the 1991 Baptist Hymnal.

Pillsbury Music Center, 1974

MABEE CENTER FOR PHYSICAL EDUCATION (1980)

On December 11, 1980, the aging Brown Gymnasium was officially replaced by the Mabee Center for Physical Education with the dedicatory address presented by veteran sports broadcaster Curt Gowdy. It was deemed "one of the finest ath-

43

Grand River Chapel, 1918, 1991

letic facilities to be found in the United States."

The project, which had been launched in April of 1979, included not only the construction of the Mabee Center but also the development of the Elliot C. Spratt outdoor sports complex on the Browning campus. Because the center was constructed on the former site of the college baseball diamond, it was necessary to relocate the diamond to the north campus. Softball and soccer fields were added as well as a road through the campus named for patriarchal coach R.E. "Dad" Bowles. The total cost of the Mabee Center and the outdoor sports complex reached $4,500,000.

The Mabee Center bears the name of John and Lottie Mabee, whose Tulsa-based foundation made the project a reality. Their lead gift of $750,000 prompted other gifts, including one from the Kansas City Chiefs professional football team which held their summer training camp at William Jewell College from 1963 to 1990.

The facility was built to further heighten the college's tradition of athletic excellence. Encompassing over 90,000 square feet, the gym has a clear-span arena that includes three basketball courts sur-

rounded by a six-lane running track. An indoor Olympic-size swimming pool graces the south end of the building. Handball courts, lockers, showers, training rooms, fitness rooms, and weight rooms accentuate the flexibility of the building, which can seat up to 1,600 spectators for a sporting event. The facility also is the site of college commencement ceremonies.

FROM WHENCE WE CAME: GRAND RIVER CHAPEL (1918, 1991)

A project of the Alumni Commission for Religious Life 1988-1992, the Grand River Chapel stands as a monument to the roots of William Jewell College. It began with the founding of the Grand River Baptist Church in December, 1833, in the northern section of what was then called Ray County and now is incorporated into southern Daviess County. Their third building, constructed in 1918, stands on the campus of William Jewell College as the Grand River Chapel.

The Grand River Baptist Church had established several churches and associations, and provided regular gifts to the Ministerial Education fund at William Jewell College during its 158-year history. When their building was given to the college, the project was accepted by the Alumni Commission to move the well-constructed 45' x 45' building to the campus as a reminder that the college was founded and supported by small rural

Baptist congregations throughout its history. The structure was dismantled piece by piece and board by board, moved to the campus by the Billings Construction Company and rebuilt under their leadership.

To finance the project, the Alumni Commission for Religious Life dedicated parts of the building to friends of families and alumni who wanted to purchase a memorial for their family members. Over seventy people are honored in the pews, windows, and accoutrements of the Grand River Chapel.

Outstanding features of the building include the William Jewell stained glass window created by alums Charlie '56 and Adelle '57 Newlon depicting logos and mottoes of the college throughout its history. This 16' x 9' stained glass edifice serves as a backdrop for weddings, graduations and other rites of passage at the college. The Grand River Gardens that surround the building, a gift of Mr. and Mrs. Jim Ferrell, feature a fountain and flagstone patio. Three historical markers on the grounds note Civil War activities in Liberty and on the Hill. The building is used by numerous campus groups, including Sigma Epsilon Pi, a campus organization for ministry students, and for community weddings.

WHITE SCIENCE CENTER (1992)

On October 11, 1992, the White Science Center was formally dedicated, capping off the most vigor-

ous fund-raising program in the history of William Jewell College. The center, costing $7,500,000, was the major capital project in a campaign that netted over $27 million toward capital and endowment functions of the college. The building replaced historic Marston Hall, built in 1914 as the science center of the campus, and provided necessary resources for the remodeling of Marston Hall.

The new 66,000-square-foot science center is a state-of-the-art facility planned by faculty members involved in teaching the sciences. Its brick con-

White Science Center, 1992

struction is compatible with the remainder of the campus, including historic Jewell Hall, its neighbor. Features of the building include twenty-three separate dedicated laboratories, a seminar conference room on the third floor, a two-tiered lecture hall, and an observatory at the highest point in Clay County and one of the highest points in Missouri. The departments of physics, chemistry, biology, computer studies, and mathematics use the facility.

The center was named for John and Penny White, alumni of the college, whose generous gift enabled the construction of the building. They reluctantly allowed their names to grace the structure if it would honor outstanding professors encountered during their studies at William Jewell College: Dr.

Murray Hunt, professor of philosophy, 1953-66; Dr. Elman Morrow, professor of mathematics and physics, 1947-68; and Dr. Kermit Watkins, professor of economics, 1956-78. A plaque of dedication is located near the quad entrance of the new building.

John F. White was born on April 4, 1944, and reared in the Maryland Baptist Children's Home in Bethesda. He attended William Jewell College at the suggestion of a Jewell graduate who directed the Home and took a special interest in young John's education. At William Jewell, White served as a student assistant in the math department and an officer in Phi Gamma Delta. During his years at the college, he met Independence native Penny Kern, the Tatler Revue Queen, who became his wife and the mother of their five children. Their son, Jason, graduated from William Jewell in 1996.

White was president of Haemonetics Corporation in Braintree, Mass. from 1983-1998. He joined the board of trustees in 1989 and assumed the chairmanship in 1993.

46

Jewell Hall, 1852

CHAPTER 4

FACULTY and ADMINISTRATION

We Will Love Thee, Serve Thee Forever

by Myra Unger

*I*n a speech to Williams College alumni on December 28, 1871, James Garfield, then leader of the Republican Party in Congress and later president of the United States, made this much-quoted statement about American higher education:

"I am not willing that this discussion should close without mention of the value of a true teacher. Give me a log hut, with only a simple bench, Mark Hopkins on one end and I on the other, and you may have all the buildings, apparatus and libraries without him."

When Garfield said this, Mark Hopkins had been president of Williams College and professor of philosophy for thirty-five years. James Garfield was one of his former students.

One of the nineteenth century's greatest orators, Garfield had graduated from Williams College with honors. One year after his graduation, at the age of twenty-six, Garfield was elected president of Western Reserve Eclectic Institute (now Hiram College), having competed with one of his own former teachers for the post. Eager to improve the quality of teaching in American colleges, Garfield lectured on American history, a new subject to col-

lege curricula; taught classes in which he encouraged students to think independently; and sponsored teacher and administrative training workshops. Garfield cared about good teaching and knew it when he saw it.

By the time of Williams' speech William Jewell's faculty, administration, trustees, and students had been struggling to shape the college for over twenty years. Lack of money and the Civil War had kept the college closed for nine of those years. We can only imagine the energy (not to mention the odor) when students and faculty together shoveled out Jewell Hall, a hospital for federal troops as well as quarters for soldiers and horses during the war, so that classes could resume on September 29, 1868.

Since then the heart of William Jewell College, as that of any other college that matters, has been its faculty, aided by the administration and staff who support and complement classroom teaching.

Professor Thurston F. Isley, Dr. Frank G. Edson, Miss Virginia D. Rice, and Dr. U.R. Pugh celebrating a total of 142 years of teaching at William Jewell, 1965

Changes in teaching techniques, philosophies, styles, and technologies may not be readily apparent to first-year students. They tend to think of a

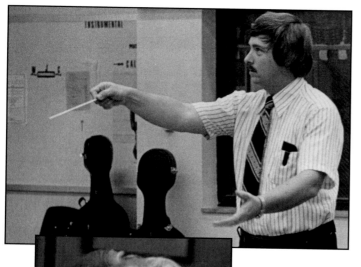

Phil Posey conducts the orchestra, 1974

Georgia B. Bowman, communication, 1974

faculty member as opening a hinged student head and putting in an ice-cream scoop of math or French, then moving on to the next student to repeat the operation.

In the prize-winning documentary, *Why Man Creates*, a hand opens such a head and yells into its emptiness, "Hello down there." The greeting echoes, but there is no response.

Opening a head and opening a mind have little in common, though. Opening a mind requires constant intellectual growth and adaptation from a faculty member. The art of teaching has changed dramatically over the last fifty years, the period this discussion focuses on. Females are no longer a tiny minority but a dynamic presence in the faculty and administration. The campus abounds with workshops, meetings, and seminars designed to enhance teaching skills as increasing emphasis is placed on assessment and outcome. Global teaching and learning are a reality due to the ease of travel and the relative security of Western Europe and Japan. Faculties have worked together in interdisciplinary programs, including the relatively new general education core curriculum. Faculty and administration members grow and evolve just as students do.

"There is no teaching until the pupil is brought into the same state or principle in which you are; a transfusion takes place; he is you and you are he; then is a teaching, and by no unfriendly chance or bad company can he ever quite lose the benefit."

–Ralph Waldo Emerson

Listen to the conversation at any college class reunion or alumni function, and among the old tales of marbles rolling down the aisle in Gano Chapel or midnight rendez-vous in the cemetery will be talk of faculty members who made a difference in the way students learned and looked at their world after graduation. Ruth Edwards' and Jeanne Johnson's advising; Katherine and Antonio Vera's teaching of Spanish via the lively Danforth Method; Nano Nore's teaching of painting or David Johnson's demonstrations of calligraphy; Sally Powers' patience in teaching learning skills; Phil Posey's encouraging students to participate in community music; Sandra Emig's dozens of music department-related projects; Gordon Kingsley's teaching of Irish poetry and drama; Lois Anne and Kim Harris' labors in journalism and drama: these are a few out of many possible examples.

Listen to the conversations of faculty members and you will sometimes hear about those moments when the mind of teacher and student met and connected in what Dr. Ann Marie Shannon calls the "intimacy of shared experience—the opportunity to open up a world and begin to inhabit it together."

Great teachers work hard at helping students inhabit their worlds, such as Dr. Shannon's world of King Lear and John Donne's sonnets. In her Survey of British Literature classes Dr. Shannon used to give "forced decision" quizzes. Her class writings were returned with comments meant to evoke dialogue and, often, office conferences. Her philosophy was as follows: "Inhabiting" a work of literature requires careful reading skills. The class discussion grows directly out of this focused thinking the students had done on paper. Every aspect of class is part of a carefully structured whole, every part reinforcing every other part so that class members find themselves inside the text. They grow confident in their own skills.

Professor Charles Newlon, "Charlie" to the campus, taught the skills necessary to "inhabit" the natural environment. Many graduates fondly recall crawling around muddy creek bottoms with Professor Newlon looking for frogs. "His enthusiasm for the natural world was so infectious," a former student said, "I felt touched with wonder, and I've never gotten over it."

Students in Dr. Wallace Hilton's physics courses also felt wonder as Dr. Hilton demonstrated—often

on equipment he had made from donated castoffs—some physics principle. He almost danced around the equipment as he demonstrated principles of gravity, inertia, or torque. His delight was compounded when his students' hands went up for further information. Among those hands were those of his successor-to-be, Dr. Don Geilker, whose own delight in "shared experiences" brings community members, as well as students, to the Pillsbury Observatory atop the White Science Center to view comets, eclipses, or Saturn's rings.

Lifelong joy of learning is the result of the "intimacy of shared experiences" fostered by great teachers. The opportunity for students and faculty to spend intense, focused time together on an ongoing basis is virtually unique to the college world, and a benefit not sufficiently stressed in college catalogs.

If teacher and student have shared experiences, they are both learners, one from the other. The teacher learns from the taught.

Elaine Reynolds, history, lecturing in 1988

D. Dean Dunham, Jr., English, 1963

Mark Walters, Professor of the Year, 1994

Gordon Kingsley in class, 1973

Cecelia Robinson, English, on her way to English 100, 1989

"I am not a teacher: only a fellow traveler of whom you asked the way. I pointed ahead–ahead of myself as well as of you."

–George Bernard Shaw

As faculty instructional aide, Dr. D. Dean Dunham, Jr. has helped both new and experienced faculty in an ongoing series of seminars to "point ahead" in thinking about the nature of teaching: what constitutes effective teaching, how one can learn the skills to do it well, where one can go for help with specific problems, and how the faculty member's own status as "learner" can improve the teaching-learning process. And he has served as the confidential, caring mentor of numerous faculty struggling to keep up with the demands of faculty life. All this plus classes and conferences with students in his literature classes. "The best teacher is a coach," Dunham once said, "not an oracle."

Such fellow travelers are often role models for their students. "I've never seen him out of control, even when he was very, very frustrated," said one of Fred Flook's former baseball players. "He was a great example." Another noted, "He could get guys to do things on a baseball field they didn't know they could do. He pulled ability out of us from somewhere and we had it ever after. We even believed we had it."

A former student described his relationship with Drs. D.O. Moore and Oscar Brooks, members of the religion department, who also believed deeply in student potential. "D.O. Moore and Oscar Brooks gave me a sense of moving out of adolescence and into adulthood. They taught me their personal planks of living. They took interest in me, spent an inordinate amount of time asking me about my concerns and interests, and this has continued since my graduation." Such encouragement extends beyond faculty members in the classroom.

Former "re-entry" students often make similar comments about the work of Dean Johnnie Human and her programs for students who wanted to return to college but were desperately worried about their ability to do the quality of work necessary. She persuaded these students to give up cowardliness for courage, and many are making significant contributions in their communities today because she convinced them they, too, could do the work. As the nineteenth-century novelist George Eliot (Marian Evans Cross) said, "If youth is the season of hope, it is often so only in the sense that our elders are hopeful about us."

Professor Richard Harriman has offered a different kind of hope to the campus and the Kansas City community: the hope that a world-class Fine Arts Program would collectively bring about cultural growth and enriched artistic sensibilities for the whole Kansas City metropolitan area. Who could ever measure the extent of his positive impact in the area? He sees himself as a fellow-traveler delighted to be along on the world-class series of fine arts events he has shepherded over the years. He is modest about his own role as impresario.

"Learning without wisdom is a load of books on a donkey's back."

–Zora Neale Hurston, 1939
(paraphrase of a Japanese proverb)

The pursuit of wisdom and Dr. Robert Trotter seemed virtually synonymous at William Jewell College for many years. Discussion in his seminar (and those of his fellow philosopher and friend, Dr. Keith David) moved quietly along as Trotter made connections and kept conversational balls in the air. Opinions were weighed and discussed, but, as one philosophy alum observed, "He never put anybody down in the classroom." He saw the classroom as his center of service and influence to the college. Sometimes he moved that classroom to his own living room where he and his wife, Juanita, served cookies and tea while students listened to classical music, viewed the Trotters' art collection, and talked about the philosophy of art.

Faculty and administration members from past years remembered for their wise counsel and sound decision-making include: P. Caspar Harvey and "Daddy" Fruit; Ruth McDaniel; Paul McCarty and Wilbur Bruner; Ed Lakin and Wes Forbis; John Davis and R.E. "Dad" Bowles; Austen Edwards; Lon Amick; Olive Thomas; Opal Carlin; F.M. Derwacter; Thurston Isley and U.R. Pugh.

It was said of Dr. Bruce Thomson that he combined "eye-to-eye honesty with long-range vision." Wisdom cannot be taught, but it can be modeled.

Dr. Jim Tanner's and Dr. Ken Chatlos' joint "Introduction to Oxbridge" seminars provide a modeling experience for initiates to the Oxbridge program. Their challenge to read carefully and write thoughtfully, using carefully gleaned and shaped arguments, is for many the first introduction to what the real "life of the mind" can be. Central to this introduction is the character of their teaching: prodding, cajoling, commenting, and cheerleading new adventures of the mind. "The mind is an enchanted thing," wrote poet Marianne Moore. It is, indeed.

Dr. Frank Edson, chemistry, 1972

Lutie Chiles, education, 1963

Ann Marie Shannon, English, and Oxbridge Senior Tutor, 1988

"Education is what survives when what has been learnt has been forgotten."

–B.F. Skinner

H.I. Hester off to golf, 1948

Bruce Thompson at work, 1966

Dr. Frank Edson, longtime chair of the chemistry department, was once chagrined when the two highest grades on an organic chemistry exam were 52 and 60 (out of 100). "I'll give you two weeks to review these chapters and prepare for another test on the same material," he told the class. Knowing Dr. Edson's rigor, the students reviewed and quaked fearfully for two weeks. On the day of the make-up exam Dr. Edson walked into the room just as the bell rang, placed two reams of paper on the front desk, and said, "Tell me everything you know about these chapters."

Twenty-five years later one of those students said, "I've always wondered: What was Dr. Edson really thinking? Was he cackling underneath his breath? Once I got over my shock (for a moment I forgot everything I knew), I began pulling material together in ways I never had before. The tests came back with comments from Dr. Edson written all over them, as if he had taken our tries at synthesis very seriously. The experience made me think differently about the way pieces of knowledge go together to form a whole after that."

Long before there was much talk of "critical thinking" on campus, Dr. Georgia Bessie Bowman was teaching her debate squads and communication classes to distinguish the clear from the garbled and to analyze and synthesize efficiently. She taught a whole collection of skills now considered the essence of critical thinking. Her insistence on practicing those skills until they were perfected produced scores of formidable public speakers and clear thinkers.

Committed to clear thinking and writing, Dr. Herman P. Wilson taught students to explicate Milton's *Paradise Lost* and James' *The Ambassadors*. He wanted students to read the words as they were written in context, and not to begin interpreting until they understood perfectly what was literally happening on that page. "What do the words on the page say?" he would ask, more than once, if necessary—and wait patiently for the response. The habit of close reading thus learned carried over into the study of other subjects as well.

A graduate sums up the education that survives: "I never felt that I was totally isolated in my discipline. My teachers were always interested in holistic problem solving. It has served me well throughout life."

"A teacher affects eternity; he can never tell where his influence ends."

–Henry Brooks Adams

Dr. H.I. Hester was a little man with a huge soul and spirit, prodigious energy, a ready wit and only minor vices, a friend of half the people in Liberty, and the writer of more than twenty books (among them two William Jewell histories on which the writers of the present book have relied heavily).

He was a seminary trustee, a co-founder (with Dr. Walter Pope Binns) of the Association of Southern Baptist Colleges and Universities, and a longtime professor of religion, as well as college vice president and interim president.

Like Mark Hopkins, both faculty member and administrator, Dr. Hester considered himself merely a steward on earth of the prodigious gifts God had given him. He believed in quiet charity. Lectureships, the H.I. Hester Alumni House, and numerous scholarships and other bequests continue the legacy of one often described by those who knew him as "a Christian gentleman," a man of towering character whose mere presence in a room raised the level of both integrity and laughter.

The past, the present, and the future overlap in a college:

- in generations of school children taught by teachers taught at William Jewell College by Miss Lutie Chiles and Miss Ella Davidson and successive members of the education department;
- in Liberty residents watching Dr. Burt Wagenknecht bicycling to collect cans on Saturday morning, earning money to be turned into cash for a biology department project;
- in eager audiences of children as Dr. Marvin Dixon gave his many performances or taught Saturday morning classes to fourth graders;
- in the wider community of Dr. Ed Chasteen's Hate

Busters or Earl Whaley's tours and ethnic meals;
- in the Kansas City community's hearing Dr. Arnold Epley direct the K.C. Symphony Chorus or Professor Terri Teal direct the Fine Arts Chorale of Kansas City;
- in the rich nationwide influence on college science teaching of Project Kaleidoscope, in which Dr. Judy Dilts has long been involved;
- in the audiences for the books and articles of faculty members across the disciplines from history and religion, English and communication, psychology and mathematics, to biology, physics, languages, and music;
- in those encouraged by the Pryor Leadership Studies Program, directed by Dr. Sylvia Nadler, to develop community problem-solving techniques;
- in community members who, attending a William Jewell College sporting event, catch something of the spirit of the place from coaches and encourage

Wallace Hilton, physics, 1973

The biology department— (from left) Nelson Scottgale, Judy Dilts, Gwen Scottgale, Burt Wagenknecht, Charles Newlon, 1991

Lydia Lovan at the organ, 1963

their children to "check out" the college when it is time to apply for college admission;

• in those who, hearing a presentation at a conference on medical ethics by Dr. Keith David, decide to sign organ donor cards;

• in voters in surrounding communities to which Dr. Will Adams' Institute for Social Research reached out in assessing voting trends;

• in Kansas City, where Dr. Cecelia Robinson's letter-writing projects, uniting inner-city children with those in the suburbs, build bridges of friendship;

• in clinics and assessments run by members of the Nursing Department for the long-term health benefits of the community;

• in England, Europe, Japan and other locations where the overseas study programs (and Oxbridge) extend the connections with different modes of learning and new aspects of culture;

• in generations of students, community members, and school groups who caught the contagion of good drama from Professor Virginia D. Rice and kept this exuberance throughout life;

• in people from "all over" who came to know the college because of William Jewell College's countless music contests and musical productions;

• in churches near and far to whom Jerry Cain and religion and music faculty have ministered;

• in faculty members and administrators whose collective stewardship of time, talent, and resources provides an inspiring legacy.

"Leadership and learning are indispensable to each other."

–John Fitzgerald Kennedy

"In the space age the most important space is between the ears."

–Anne Armstrong

Like all viable organisms, a college and its faculty and administration evolve if they are to survive. They grow to meet the challenges. When James Garfield said, "Give me a log hut, with only a simple bench, Mark Hopkins on one end and I on the other," Garfield was not suggesting that a college can do without "buildings, apparatus, and libraries" (or stadiums, all-purpose tracks, snack bars, art galleries, and heating plants, as well as all of the folks who make these work). Mark Hopkins, in his dual role, was teaching students, while helping administer the "buildings, apparatus, and libraries." Garfield was simply reminding colleges to look to the essential: the Mark Hopkins' in dialogue with students. The results of such dialogue are a college's legacy.

CHAPTER 5

ACADEMIC LIFE

The Cause of Our Existence

by Ann Marie Shannon

When the first William Jewell College *Catalogue* was published in 1849, it listed "Trustees, Teachers," announced that the first session was "to commence on the First Day of January, 1850," and identified the frontier location of the new college as "Liberty, Clay County." Most significant of all, its modest statement of "Course of Study, &c. &c." placed William Jewell squarely on the spacious intellectual landscape it has inhabited for 150 years.

Strictly speaking, the *Catalogue* did not list a course of study. Rather, it listed a faculty and identified the subjects of their teaching: "Ancient Languages" and "Mathematics and Natural Sciences." Some early marketing strategy was demonstrated: "Should the number of Students require it, additional Teachers will be immediately engaged." It is important to note that the faculty would need enlargement only when there were too many students for two men to instruct. No need was anticipated for additional subjects. "Ancient Languages" and "Mathematics and Natural Sciences" constituted a curriculum rich enough for a full education in 1849.

The original readers of this historic announcement would have understood that study of "Ancient Languages" involved not only Latin and Greek grammar but also the ancient world's history and literature, including the New Testament. If "Ancient Languages" implied a broad study of culture and religious faith, so "Natural Sciences" would have implied equal breadth of study of the physical world and mathematics. Jewell's original curriculum combined both abstract intellectual systems and the very practical application of those systems to frontier commerce and the surveying of new land.

A hundred and fifty years later, a reader who translates the deceptively brief statement into formal terms will see that William Jewell's early

The first Catalogue

CATALOGUE
of the
TRUSTEES, TEACHERS
COURSE OF STUDY, &c. &c.
of
William Jewell College,
located in
LIBERTY, CLAY COUNTY, MO.
First Session to commence the First Day of January,
1850.
PRINTED AT THE OFFICE OF
THE WESTERN MISSOURI WEEKLY EXPRESS.
1849.

The Twentieth-Century Academician, Dr. Kingsley, 1980-1993

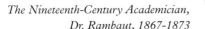

The Nineteenth-Century Academician, Dr. Rambaut, 1867-1873

THE "ACADEMICIANS"

Two of the presidents who have served the college in the past 150 years have been notably important in articulating Jewell's liberal arts identity. One is Dr. Thomas Rambaut, who came to Jewell when it reopened after the Civil War. He gave the "Course of Study" a formal structure which shaped academics for nearly a century. The first chapter of this sesquicentennial history aptly names him William Jewell's "Academician." A hundred years later, one of his successors, Dr. J. Gordon Kingsley, initiated a revitalization of Dr. Rambaut's structure which could earn him the designation as Jewell's "Twentieth-Century Academician."

academic life comprised the study of humanities, social science, science and mathematics, and religion. Thus, the first *Catalogue* established a pattern of study that has persisted throughout every period of the college's life and is reaffirmed by the current *Catalog*. This inclusive pattern of study identified William Jewell as what today is called a "liberal arts college" and defined its place on the academic landscape. Small colleges like Jewell represent America's unique contribution to higher education.

THE RAMBAUT LEGACY

Dr. H.I. Hester's history, *Jewell Is Her Name*, admirably traces Dr. Rambaut's achievement. Identifying a wide range of subjects to be studied and organizing them into groups, he produced a coherent, if overly ambitious, curriculum modeled after that of the University of Virginia. He proposed eight "schools": Latin, Greek, mathematics, modern languages, English literature and history, natural sciences, moral philosophy, and theology. Each school was to be independent of the others. Graduation was to depend on examinations, not any given period of study.

The strength shown in Dr. Rambaut's academic plan was not educational imagination or originality. It was, rather, recognition and vigorous adaptation of the best educational practice of the time. Appropriating it for William Jewell, he gave the college a framework around which it could build its academic progress. That framework supported Jewell's expanded and enriched academic life from the Civil War until World War II dramatically changed American life, including higher education.

Over the years these original courses were regrouped and the graduation requirements modified. Progressive regrouping through the decades ultimately produced the now familiar twentieth-century categories.

Even these progressive changes, however, were modifications of Dr. Rambaut's original model. Jewell, in common with most other American institutions, later rejected the examination-based system for earning degrees and abandoned Rambaut's provision for the master's degree. However, the subdivision of courses of study, the grouping of subjects, and the requirement for study of a range of subjects from different groups established the liberal arts framework. The organization of groups into independent "schools" paved the way for academic departments as we know them today.

Within this firmly established departmental

Cadets march to class

Aircraft engines class for naval cadets

framework, new subjects appeared steadily in the *Catalogs* which followed Dr. Rambaut's retirement in 1873. They provided specialization and elaboration within the broad fields of knowledge his plan identified. Further expansion brought lively activities such as debate, dramatics, and musical performance into the formal curriculum.

Physical training for naval cadets

WAR YEARS: WORLD WAR II AND THE VETERANS' INVASION

The impact of another conflict ended the long period of growth which Dr. Rambaut initiated in the years following the Civil War. After the United States entered World War II in December, 1941, and men of traditional college age went into military service, the college continued to offer its regular academic program to a student body made up increasingly of young women. In addition, however, cadets from two naval aviation pro-

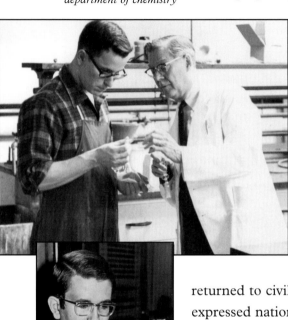

Dr. Frank Edson (right), chair, department of chemistry

Physics, 1972

grams brought a military presence to the campus.

From 1942 to 1945, 2,980 men of the Naval Flight Preparatory School marched in formation to classes preparing them for flight training. Jewell faculty members were among their civilian instructors. In 1944, Jewell became one of eight sites for a Naval Academic Refresher Unit (V 5). Seven hundred men preparing to be pilots reported to Marston Hall for courses in mathematics, physics, English, and history taught by a special faculty employed by the college.

When the war ended and the thousands of military veterans returned to civilian life, the U.S. Congress expressed national gratitude for their service by enacting the legislation popularly named the "GI Bill" to provide benefits to men and women honorably discharged from the armed forces. Important educational benefits provided not only for job training but also for college study. Tuition grants, which were substantial for their time, and modest monthly living allowances made higher education or advanced professional study available to people who before the war could never have dreamed of "going to college."

Enrollments soared in schools across America as the returning vets invaded. Jewell *Catalogs* from

1945-46 through the 1950s included sections on "William Jewell College and Veterans," reporting that at the beginning of the period veterans made up approximately half of the student body. Their enrollment in significant proportions continued through the '50s, when GI benefits were extended to veterans of the Korean conflict.

These *Catalogs* also detail the generous efforts of the college to help veterans make the transition to academic life, including a Veterans Advisory Committee and the offer of "reasonable" credit for experiences in the service. In other words, they testify to William Jewell's energetic participation in an important enlargement of higher education.

The vets' invasion lent a concretely human dimension to the powerful movements which renewed American college life in the time of rebuilding after World War II. The influential 1945 report of the Harvard Committee, *General Education in a Free Society*, signaled these changes as it gave a specific name to "graduation requirements" and coherently defined their purpose. "The Harvard Report" inaugurated a period of increasing emphasis on general education, especially interdisciplinary learning and core curricula. The idea that education was a weapon in the Cold War encouraged experimental projects. The turmoil of the 1960s provoked debate about the proper role of students in determining their educational experiences. But before and through those years of unrest, innovation in both curriculum and instructional methods characterized American colleges.

THE ACADEMIC CRISIS

Though William Jewell shared the veterans' return, it was largely unaffected by the movements of curricular and instructional change. Alumni of the '40s, '50s, and '60s remember with gratitude the vital learning they experienced with individual teachers in particular courses. However, there was little attention to the curriculum as a whole. By the end of the 1960s, the result was an academic crisis clearly outlined in the reports of the accrediting organization, the North Central Association of Colleges and Secondary Schools.

William Jewell was first accredited by North Central in 1915, shortly after that body was established. The college is justifiably proud of having maintained its accreditation consistently since, with the only qualification being a three-year period of private probation from 1968-1971. After institution of the current system of self-study followed by formal review, Jewell went through the process in 1959, 1968, 1971, 1981, and 1991. The next review is scheduled for 2001.

The 1959 reviewers found Jewell a "good college" and continued accreditation for the maximum period. They expressed some academic concerns, however, especially that the "academic side of life at William Jewell appears to be controlled largely if not entirely by the various departments without much coordinating effort or action." They were

Pryor Leadership Fellows: Outward Bound trip— high ropes course, 1995

especially troubled by the effect on general education.

North Central intensified these concerns, with others, in the 1968 review, which resulted in private probation—that is, probation without public announcement by the association. As explained in the first chapter of this history, the reviewers' heaviest indictment fell on the college's administrative structure, but they also detailed serious academic weaknesses. These included a low percentage of faculty doctorates, a small instructional budget, heavy teaching and advisory loads, and low faculty salaries. Reviewers quoted student complaints about lecture as the primary instructional method and absence of "meaningful discussion, even in the smaller classes." Their criticism of the general curriculum was especially severe. They emphasized that "there are not college-wide curricular studies underway and no long-range studies have been projected."

59

Natural history II field trip

Dr. Wallace A. Hilton, physics

The president of Jewell's board of trustees left a candid memorandum of his meeting with North Central officials in hopes "of getting some less devastating word or words" than "probation" for "our time of testing." He reported that the officials were "hospitable and cordial" but unrelenting in the opinion that the review had been "charitable." He concluded ruefully that it was "nothing new" for accreditors "to see trustees writhe in discomfort."

Even today, it is difficult not to writhe at the forthright language used in the meeting to describe "academic deficiencies at William Jewell." According to the memo, the officials noted that the "curriculum appears to be too fragmented and static—it must be dynamic and under constant scrutiny." They concluded: "Looks like . . . a good sales program but we fear . . . not a very good product to sell."

At the end of the three-year probationary period, a rigorous 1971 review restored Jewell to normal accreditation. However, the reviewers pointed out that because their report recorded results of a special review, "it necessarily focused on negative aspects." Their sternest words defined "An interesting educational paradox": spokesmen for the college "proffer great interest in 'making certain the college is preparing citizens for today's world'—and simultaneously they try to accomplish this task within the patterns of a disappearing educational structure."

The report thus pointed toward the end of the long period when Dr. Rambaut's structure would be adequate for William Jewell's educational needs. In addition, however, it pointed toward a new model for the future. In concluding that "William Jewell is basically a good college" with a focus "which augurs well for its future," the reviewers based strong hopes on the newly appointed "Achievement '70s" committee made up of ten faculty members, three students, and three administrators, and chaired by "a very able and energetic young professor of English."

THE KINGSLEY INITIATIVES

This committee of some of the strongest members of the campus community set to work on a task that was nothing less than examining the whole educational program of the college. The young English professor who chaired them was Dr. J. Gordon Kingsley, shortly to become associate dean, then later dean of the college and eventually president. Bringing to the project a powerfully creative educational imagination, he led in designing the program known as "Achievement '70s: Education for Individual Achievement." After thorough debate, the faculty approved the program as a whole in 1972.

According to the self-study report prepared before the next North Central review, "Achievement '70s" "had a large symbolic impact on campus, bringing with it a spirit of renewal and a sense of academic purpose somewhat larger than the actual changes effected in daily operations." Those changes were notable, however, many of them assimilating innovations which had renewed post-war American education. Changes included a revised academic calendar with a short "Winterim" term in January for creative experimental courses; encouragement of independent study, honors projects, and self-designed majors; overseas study; and a revitalized advisory process stressing the individual educational goals of the student and making advising a formal obligation in each faculty contract.

Dr. Kingsley personally traveled abroad to lead the extension of Jewell's hilltop into a world campus. As a result, the first Jewell students went in 1973 to Harlaxton, the British campus of the University of Evansville, to be succeeded every year since by Jewell students and faculty who have lived, studied, and taught in the ornate manor house. Also in 1973, the first students went to Regent's Park, the Baptist College of Oxford University. The next years extended opportunities in Oxford through a private program, the Oxford Overseas Study Course, and the most recent addition allows them access to the Centre for Medieval and Renaissance Studies affiliated with Keble College. An exchange program with Seinan Gakuin University in Japan began in 1975. By the end of the 1970s, overseas opportunities also included Jewell's own summer program in Spain, cooperative arrangements in Europe, and agreements with colleges of Cambridge University, first Wolfson and then Homerton.

Nearly thirty years later, Jewell students have opportunity to study in some two dozen overseas programs in England, France, Germany, Austria, Italy, Spain, India, Israel, Australia, Southeast Asia, Japan, the Caribbean, and Central and South America.

One unique relative of this rich international enterprise is the Oxbridge Honors Program of Tutorial Majors, begun in 1984 after four years of discussion and planning. Oxbridge, which gets its name from the colloquial British fusion of Oxford and Cambridge, embodies Dr. Kingsley's long-dreamed-of design of British-style tutorial instruction on an American campus. Endowed by a grant of $1,050,000 from the Hall Family Foundations, Oxbridge allows a few carefully

World Campus: Harlaxton

World Campus: Paris

William Jewell students try their hand at crew in Oxford, England.

selected students to pursue specially designed tutorial majors while doing the rest of their work in traditional American classes. They spend the junior year in one of Jewell's programs in Oxford or Cambridge, returning to campus for senior comprehensive examinations.

Just as Dr. Rambaut's structural plan served as a framework for further developments, so "Achievement '70s" created a curricular environment open to new, often untraditional programs. Recent products of this environment have emphasized leadership and humanitarian service and, like Oxbridge, have attracted outside funding.

For example, the Service Learning Program allows a student to earn a certificate by combining theoretical courses with service projects and internships in community organizations. A recent gift of $1,500,000 from an anonymous donor will support the program and make possible establishment of a Service Learning Center especially concerned with issues important to women.

The Pryor Leadership Studies Program also combines theory with practical experience to develop "personal, vocational and civic leadership." The Certificate program for Pryor Leadership Fellows–which includes classes, internships, and a rigorous Outward Bound trip–was established in

1993 in conjunction with the Pryor Foundation, headed by alumni Fred and Shirley Pryor.

The most encompassing "Achievement '70s" program was the most controversial and difficult to accomplish–the move toward a contemporary interdisciplinary core for general education. The "Achievement '70s" committee wearily reported in 1972 that they "labored more on the general education program" than on any other matter, but could reach no agreement. They recommended further "experimentation and deliberation" to develop an interdisciplinary pilot by fall 1972 "or as soon thereafter as possible." Though the faculty approved the proposal, no specific program gained approval.

In 1978, Dr. Kingsley, then dean, appointed a new faculty general education committee. After nineteen months of intense work, in constant consultation with the faculty, it designed the "Foundations for the Future" core for introduction into the curriculum in 1981. A consultant/reviewer from the National Endowment for the Humanities observed, "I know of no comparable effort accomplished so methodically, so thoroughly, or so well."

In catalog language, Foundations provided "an integrated value-based study of public and private decision making, relating Christian heritage and cultural past to contemporary problems," including social and scientific issues. The rigorous core of six team-taught courses was offered to approximately sixty new students each year as a voluntary alternative to the traditional distribution system of departmental courses. With developments and changes, this "two-track" system has been durable to the present. It will be phased out by the turn of the century, however, to be supplanted by a new core curriculum for all students.

Beginning with the entering class of 1996, students began taking first-year courses in written and oral communication, mathematical model building, foreign language or an equivalent, and physical education. Their common interdisciplinary course is "The Responsible Self," a humanities course in which they wrestle with questions of responsibility from different cultural and ideological perspectives. At level two, they choose from a variety of interdisciplinary courses in "Culture and Traditions" (humanities), "Power and Justice in Society" (social sciences), "Science, Technology and the Human Experience" (science, including lab), and "Sacred and Secular" (religious studies). As juniors or seniors they bring their general education experience together in a capstone course. They will thus extend the influence of "Achievement '70s" into a new century.

"Achievement '70s" affirmed the commitment of the college's mission statement to "provide sound liberal arts education." However, in the understanding of "liberal arts," an ambiguity remained which increasingly required clarification. This was the tendency of more and more Americans to regard higher education primarily as

preparation for careers. Jewell has had to battle an ethic that rejects learning for its own sake, and for personal development, as an impractical luxury.

The dichotomy would have seemed strange to the founders who published Jewell's first "Course of Study." They would not have used the term "liberal arts," of course, but they assumed that classical learning brought personal fulfillment while also benefiting the practical intelligence needed to cope with frontier life. However, as twentieth-century *Catalogs* began to publish statements articulating the college's "aims," they contrasted liberal education as personal development with practical application in professional study. The contrast was between "making a living" and "making a life." They typically made a connection, however, by describing the liberal arts as good preparation for postgraduate professional work.

Art, 1994

The contrast was also evident in the curriculum. *Catalogs* from the 1930s onward outline ways courses could best be selected to provide good preparation for medical or law school. Cooperative "three-two" programs were established to allow students to combine three years of study at Jewell with two years of engineering or forestry at schools such as Washington University or Duke. Early *Catalogs* included journalism courses or listed Kansas City-Western Dental College as an extension department. Teacher education courses appeared in the World War I era and a "composite" economics-business major was announced for 1946-47. Nursing was added in 1970 and computer studies in the 1980s. Deliberately focused professional education, however, was most strongly facilitated by the first offering of the Bachelor of Science degree in 1968.

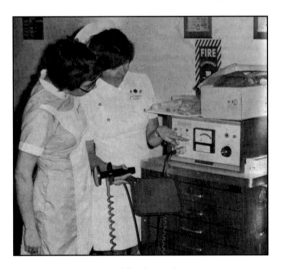

Nursing, 1976

After the 1981 review, the North Central report succinctly summarized the cumulating effect of these developments on Jewell's academic life. The report noted "a significant drop" in liberal arts majors and corresponding increase in B.S. professional areas. "While these facts indicate that the college is meeting the career needs of its students," it concluded, "the situation should be re-assessed as the institution plans for the future" and "an important element of future long range planning should be concern for the liberal arts component."

Reflecting on the relation of professional studies to the liberal arts did become a focus of the next planning activity. In 1989, Dr. Kingsley appointed an "Achievement '90s" committee to survey the whole educational effort of the college. It articulated the significant academic decision facing the college as a choice between being a liberal arts college or a "comprehensive" institution "starring" a few strong professional programs. A faculty "straw poll" favored the former, but the issue continued to be debated after President Kingsley appointed a new planning committee to prepare the college for the next millennium. That committee proposed "some bold initiatives" in the report which it issued in August of 1993, *Leadership 2000: Choices*. The report expressed strong commitment to the liberal arts, "with a practical understanding of the role of the liberal arts in career development," primarily as preparation for postgraduate study. Actions proposed included elimination of the Bachelor of Science degree; encouragement of all students majoring in professional areas to obtain second majors in traditional liberal arts subjects; and limitation of the maximum number of hours in any major, which would in practice curtail or even eliminate some professional programs.

Following Dr. Kingsley's retirement in the fall of 1993, the trustees did not take action on *Leadership 2000*. The questions it had raised about professional studies in a liberal arts college remained unanswered.

THE SESQUICENTENNIAL AND BEYOND

Answering those questions–along with others about the relation of liberal arts, religious faith, and Baptist heritage–was an essential task of the strategic planning steering committee appointed by President W. Christian Sizemore in 1995, at the

Dr. David O. Moore, religion

close of his first year in office. Discussions with many constituencies within the college community, the most thorough market research ever undertaken by the college, and careful analysis of both experience and philosophy by a subcommittee of the planning group produced the conclusions offered in *The Strategic Plan: 1997.* This plan was endorsed by the trustees at their 1997 June meeting.

This important document clarifies Jewell's position as a liberal arts college which can incorporate professional studies because it connects them to liberal arts programs and "connects liberal learning with preparation for work." It goes further to state Jewell's willingness "to undertake study of the possibility of offering . . . a few master's programs in professional areas which can be closely connected to the liberal arts." The plan makes clear, however, that such programs will never be instituted if they compromise the college's essential commitment to undergraduate liberal arts education.

This liberal arts identity issue settled in *The Strategic Plan* is articulated in the competitive strategy developed through the planning process and approved by the board of trustees in February, 1997: "William Jewell will seek a preeminent position in the Midwest for academic programs, curricula, and learning opportunities distinguished by the connections they make, particularly between liberal learning and professional competence, for students' holistic development."

Dr. Robert Trotter, philosophy

This strategy returns William Jewell's academic life to the spirit of the first *Catalogue*. The vision statement of the 1997 plan describes Jewell as "the college founded one hundred and fifty years ago on the mid-continent's western frontier . . . a . . . liberal arts college . . . committed to connecting education which enhances a person's intellectual and spiritual life with practical application in work and service." The academic life of the hilltop campus thus remains located on the intellectual landscape of its origins.

CHAPTER 6

STUDENT LIFE

Deep Within Our Hearts She Dwells

by Neita Geilker

*F*or the first few decades of student life, opportunities for activities were limited and not considered essential to a balanced college experience.

In contrast, by the 1990s, student activities had become an important ingredient for the well-rounded liberal arts graduate. A recent *Student Handbook* lists forty-nine opportunities for involvement for William Jewell College students.

This chapter considers highlights of student activities as they have increased in number and importance over the years and uses representative photos to document and invite memories.

Literary Societies Offer Culture

From the 1850s to the 1920s, two literary societies, the Philomathic and the Excelsior, provided an array of cultural experiences. Meeting on Friday evenings on the divided sides of the third level of Jewell Hall, members enjoyed debates, readings, orations, music, and great literature. The annual literary society contest featuring debate, oratory, and reading was a highlight for the entire college.

Each society had its own intellectually inspiring cheer.

For the Philomathians:

> *Boomer racker, Boomer, racker,*
> *Boomer racker roi.*
> *Sis boom, firecracker,*
> *Phil est moi.*
> *Hip zoo, rah zoo, zip rah boom,*
> *We're Philomathians; Give us room.*

For the Excelsiors:

> *Haec cum Zika Boom,*
> *Zika, Zika, Zah!*
> *Excelsior, Excelsior!*
> *Rah! Rah! Rah!*

Other organizations listed in the 1920 *Tatler* include the Public Speaking Society, The Keats Club, Keen Spitters, the Buttinsky Club (to butt and boast), the Bolsheviki Club (to bring Excelsior Springs and K.C. closer to William Jewell), the

Student Volunteer Band, and the Cosmopolitan Club.

With the admission of women in 1917, women's organizations evolved. The girls' Student Government Association began in the early 1920s and functioned through 1925 when student leadership merged. And the YWA was organized at the Second Baptist Church of Liberty in 1924.

Through the 1940s, home state clubs thrived representing student contingents from Kansas, Nebraska, Oklahoma, Kentucky, Colorado, and several Northeastern states.

Students Work for Tuition

Before formal financial aid existed, many Jewell students experienced Hester Aid. When Vice President and Dean Dr. H.I. Hester faced a desperate student who loosely qualified for ministerial aid, his typical response was, "We'll find a way." Remarkably, he always did. And in the early years, even before Dr. Hester served as vice president, students were helped with their tuition through an interesting variety of jobs.

Loren Goings remembers working in the early 1930s for 20 cents an hour sweeping the dining hall in New Ely twice a week and scrubbing it on Saturdays. When olives were served, both jobs were the pits. He also remembers a couple of years of rising at 6 a.m. to fire the furnace for Ely's hot water supply.

Other students did janitorial work in Brown Gym, milked the cows, and took care of the horses stabled in a barn by the President's Home. One football player served as a chauffeur for Dr. Herget, who loved to ride horseback but often relied on students for longer automobile trips, especially to St. Louis.

One student, who maintained his worn shoes by replacing the cardboard linings each morning, was observed to disappear after serving others in the dining hall. When other student employees discovered he simply could not afford to eat, they provided him with their own version of dining hall manna each day.

Work Day a Tradition

Introduced by President Herget, and lasting into the late '40s, one Friday each spring was designated Work Day. Town students brought their own yard tools and beginning at 8 a.m., the entire campus, including both Presidents Herget and Binns, raked and curried the grounds. A picnic lunch was served to celebrate this annual rite of spring.

STUDENTS ENJOY MULTIPLE OPPORTUNITIES TO ACHIEVE

Academic achievement and outstanding leadership draw high praise and opportunities for recognition at William Jewell.

Alpha Lambda Delta Becomes Inclusive

Begun as a campus organization, the freshman

1969 Who's Who. Seated: Carol Calvin, Buck Robinson, Lyndia Massey. Standing: Catherine Winfrey, Larry Ward, Gregg Hagg, Phyllis Newman, Scott Armstrong, Stan Hixson, Chris Herring, Annette McGinnis, Larry Stone, Bob York, Paula Wallace, Richard Reiff.

women's honorary later affiliated with Alpha Lambda Delta. In the 1980s, along with the national organization, it opened its ranks to men, thus also supplanting Nu Zeta Sigma freshman honorary for men.

Its purpose is to encourage superior scholastic achievement during the freshman year, to promote intelligent living and a high standard of learning, and to assist young men and women in recognizing and developing meaningful goals for their roles in society.

To be eligible, students must carry twelve or more hours and earn a 3.5 average by the end of their first semester or maintain that cumulative average. Typically, 10 to fifteen percent of the freshman class (thirty to sixty students) are invited to join.

Aeons Select Outstanding Senior Men

This self-perpetuating organization for senior men uses GPA and campus service as selection criteria. Members are tapped at the end of their junior year. The honor is a silent one, with activities known only to members. Their existence was announced in 1905-06 in the first *Tatler: Aeons Senior Society; Founded in the class of 1906. Purpose: Best interest of William Jewell.*

Top Women Named by Panaegis

Founded in 1928, the members have dedicated themselves to serve in the best interest of William Jewell. Seven junior women were selected each year on the basis of outstanding leadership, personality, scholarship, and character and were expected to exemplify the highest qualities of womanhood throughout life.

Panaegis Affiliates with Mortarboard

In 1978, the Panaegis chapter of Mortarboard was instituted at William Jewell, thus making it coeducational. Criteria for Mortarboard include leadership, scholarship, service, and a GPA of at least 3.2.

Many Selected for *Who's Who*

Who's Who Among Students in American Colleges and Universities selects thirty to forty students annually from among the top twenty-five percent in terms of academic and extracurricular activities.

For many years, P. Caspar Harvey tracked graduates recognized in *Who's Who in America* and concluded that, on a percentage basis, William Jewell fared better than any of the Ivy League schools.

Discipline-Related Honoraries Active

Eleven national honor societies on campus are associated with a major or discipline: Alpha Psi Omega, dramatics; Beta Beta Beta, biology; Delta Mu Delta, business administration; Kappa Mu Epsilon, mathematics; Lambda Nu Sigma, law; Phi Alpha Theta, history; Phi Sigma Tau, philosophy; Pi Kappa Delta, forensics; Psi Chi, psychology; Sigma Pi Sigma, physics; Sigma Theta Tau, nursing.

Seniors Elected to Phi Epsilon

Begun in the 1930s by Dr. and Mrs. F.M. Derwacter, Phi Epsilon has become William Jewell's academic achievement award for seniors. Each year, the top 10 percent of graduating seniors are tapped, based on their overall GPA.

Faculty Confers Coveted Award

Since 1980, the faculty has selected an outstanding student to receive the Faculty Award, the highest non-degree award given to an undergraduate. To be eligible, a student must have completed all undergraduate work at William Jewell and have a GPA of at least 3.75.

Evaluating applications and personal essays, a faculty committee narrows the field to three to seven finalists and selects those who demonstrate the highest ideals of a liberal arts education: academic achievement, service, leadership, and Christian commitment. Recipients receive a modest cash gift, their name on a plaque, and rousing recognition during the Honors Convocation. Prior to 1980, academic recognition was based on GPA, often with more than one senior achieving an overall 4.0.

Colonel/General Alexander Doniphan and First Lady Named

Since 1940, the campus has selected its own version of "most likely to succeed." The military title harks back to Alexander Doniphan, a war hero and legislator and clearly the most celebrated and best-known name associated with William Jewell. While Doniphan was elected a colonel in the U.S. Army by his regiment, he earned the rank of brigadier general in the Missouri State Militia. Consequently, some years saw the recipients designated as colonel and other years, general. Both Doniphan and First Lady of the Campus titles designate qualities of outstanding leadership and a potential to excel.

In 1996, recognition for the First Lady was

Faculty Award Winners	
1980-81	Andrew L. Pratt
1981-82	Jeannie Hirsch
	Steve Sites
1982-83	Christine Palacas
1983-84	Daniel H. Jones
1984-85	Andrea S. Eddy
1985-86	Tim Thompson
1986-87	Paul F. Paulter Jr.
1987-88	James E. Wooldridge
1988-89	Deborah Ward
1989-90	Mary McCormick
1990-91	Mark Hoffman
1991-92	Philip Pietroburgo
1992-93	Daniel Pearson
1993-94	Allison McLaren
1994-95	Kristin (Casey) Smith
1995-96	Holly Flora
1996-97	Agata Bednarz
1997-98	Paul Cernin

Year	Col./Gen. Alexander Doniphan		
40	Gene Hollman	70	Tom Dunn
41	Dick Quick	71	Jay Maddox
42	Jack Wilkes	72	Carl Fuller
43	Bob Shornick	73	Charles Lederer
44	Jim Stertz	74	Don Frey
45	Kermit Whiteaker	75	Ollie Malone
46	Bill Nelson	76	Larry Dickerson
47	John Truex	77	Greg Leibold
48	Charles Woodford Rixey	78	Charles Rainbolt
49	Dick Bowles	79	Jerald L. Hill
50	Don Ellenberger	80	Bob Kirkland
51	A. C. McKinney	81	Mark Blaylock
52	Bill Burkhardt	82	Brian Richards
53	John Gordon Barth	83	James Bailey
54	Bert Adams	84	Mark Mundell
55	William V. Miller	85	Brad Banning
56	Richard Byrne	86	Vernon Howard
57	Earle Dale	87	Mark Bross
58	Jack Armstrong	88	Greg Duncan
59	Jerry Curnutt	89	Craig Zahnd
60	George Arthur Carder	90	David Carder
61	David D. Burhans	91	Alan Kuykendall
62	Arthur Cunningham	92	John David Roberts
63	Denny Lambert	93	Shane Davolt
64	John Clizbe	94	Chad Jolly
65	Tom Trotter	95	Harry Cook
66	Michael Scroggin	96	Ryan O'Hara
67	Lawrence Russell Holley II	97	Rick Hankins
68	James Lyle Martin	98	Dan Kellermeyer
69	John Davis		

changed to the Leona Kresse Award in honor of the first woman graduate of William Jewell. Heather Wiley was the first to receive the new title.

Over the years, four couples who later married have been selected jointly for this honor. Additionally, three couples received the awards in sequential years: Madeline Parrott and Dick Quick; John Barth and Joan Pryor; Mark Blaylock and Jeannie Hirsch.

The one father-son pair to be named as Alexander Doniphan was the late Art Carder and David Carder. Additionally, one brother-sister pair, Dick and Polly Quick, and one sister-sister pair, Madeline and Ella Mae Parrott, received recognition.

STUDENT ACTIVITIES/COLLEGE UNION THRIVE AT JEWELL

Old Ely Was the Hub

In early years, the Student Activities Committee assumed a variety of responsibilities, including overseeing student resources in the Co-op and later the Hub.

The Co-op, begun in 1917 and initially housed in the basement of Gano Chapel, sold books as well as candy and pop. It also served as the student gathering place and provided employment for a very professional student staff. In the late '40s, the Co-op was moved to the Hub on the first floor of Old Ely, located in the center of the Quad. The Hub offered students a snack bar, modest recre-

In 1949, students selected Polly Quick Bowles and Richard P. Bowles as First Lady and General Alexander Doniphan.

ational activities, a television room, and the Co-op Bookstore.

With the construction of Yates College Union in 1958 and the accompanying rise of College Union Activities (the CUA), the Old Ely Hub was dismantled or perhaps it simply crumbled away.

Today, a self-perpetuating board and twelve council members who administer programs of cultural, educational, recreational, and social interest to students lead the CUA. In 1970, Stairs Down, a coffeehouse, opened in the lower level of Yates College Union.

Over the years, popular activities have included the all-school picnic (and water slide for the brave), the two-bit movie series, dessert at the Hyatt chocolate bar after Fine Arts performances, the Spring Fling, a ski trip during winterim, Lighting of the Quad, the all-campus activities fair, performances by popular music groups and solo artists including Toad the Wet Sprocket and Sara McLachlan, the Roe vs. Wade retrospective debate of Sarah Weddington and Phyllis Schlafley, and the 1986 visit and address of former President Jimmy Carter.

Year   First Lady

Year	First Lady	Year	First Lady
40	Madeline Parrott	68	George Ann Aull
41	Bessie Blythe Burkhardt	69	Paula Wallace
42	Elizabeth Prince	70	Donna Matthews
43	Jean Conrad	71	LuAnn Wood
44	Helen Prince	72	Nancy Hodgin
45	Penny Paynter	73	Julia Moore
46	Ella Mae Parrott	74	Carol Roberts
47	Mary Moon	75	Lorraine Fiero
48	Ruth Ellen Halter	76	Jean Elizabeth Poore
49	Polly Quick	77	Ann Cuneio
50	Mary Helen Kennedy	78	Dee Ann Henry
51	Rena Hank Leatherman	79	Lindsay Roach
52	Judith Borchers	80	Robba Addison
53	Diane Doane	81	Rebekah N. Bray
54	Joan Pryor	82	Jeannie Hirsch
55	Arvilla Neef	83	Josephine Stanton
56	Mary Ann Nance	84	Rhonda A. Barry
57	Ruth Ann Harr	85	Karen E. Edison
58	Cynthia Hirni	86	Lori Andersen
59	Carol Ann Carter	87	Sara Landers
60	Wilma Lee Grove	88	Amy Brown
61	Kaye Cokely	89	Sherrill Roberts
62	Toni Bolenbaugh	90	Kim Reser
63	Judy Miller	91	Amy Chastain
64	Linda Hanks	92	Mary Frazier
65	Sue Bayer	93	Jennifer Buffa
66	Sue Ellen Williams	94	Jean Tinning
67	Linda Kay Harger	95	Lisa Pettijohn

Year   Leona Kresse Award *(name changed from First Lady)*

Year	Leona Kresse Award
96	Heather Wiley
97	Jill Kuntz
98	Jaime Stuart

1979-80 CUA Committee Members:
Front row: Lori Burnham, Don Glidewell, Colleen Winquist, Cathy Johnson, Gretchen Metz, Robin Hollrah, Pam Meyer, Karen Allen, Mary Jo Becvar.
Second row: Mark Manglese, Mike Wilcox, Mike Parrot, Alecia Craft, Mailyn Summers, Joni Crabill, Jane Ann Goodson, Lisa Adkins, Pam Kleikamp, Lionnel Fleming, Laurie Brown, Ann Deerson.

CUA members Amy Brown and Kathy Sheppard with President Jimmy Carter, 1986.

1992-93: Christmas memories include the Hanging of the Green and the Lighting of the Quad.

Student Senate Leads Campus

Student Senate is the governing organization of the student body. Before 1931, senators elected their own officers. Today, the student body, following vigorous campaigning, elects the student body president and vice president.

Student Senate comprises class officers, representatives of recognized student organizations and, since 1980, four senators, one elected from each class. Currently, it addresses a broad array of student concerns from philosophy to politics to student grievances.

Since the early 1950s, an annual encampment has provided opportunity for creative planning and relationship building which, in addition to the Senate, has included many members of the administration as well as faculty leaders.

For many years, bright red vests, donned on meeting day, provided visibility for the senators and thus easier access by their constituents.

An early '50s dream of the Senate was a student

Tom Bray, 1949 Student Body president and chairman of Student Senate.

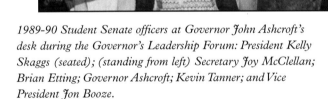

1989-90 Student Senate officers at Governor John Ashcroft's desk during the Governor's Leadership Forum: President Kelly Skaggs (seated); (standing from left) Secretary Joy McClellan; Brian Etting; Governor Ashcroft; Kevin Tanner; and Vice President Jon Booze.

handbook, now an essential resource for the entire campus. In recent years, the Senate has taken the lead in making the Union and other campus buildings smoke-free and in initiating a successful recycling program.

The Senate president now attends the board of trustee meetings.

Year	Student Body Presidents		
25	Herbert Zach		
26	T. L. Noel	63	Bob Moore
27	George Gates	64	Jim Rodewald
28	Joe Lyon	65	Mike Scrogin
29	Howard Smith	66	Jim Simmons
30	Beverly Carmichael	67	Jim Phillips
31	Douglas Rae	68	Mark Stuart
32	Scott Conway	69	Tom Dunn
33	Lowell Ditzen	70	George Flanagan
34	Bruce Summers	71	Richard Miller
35	Melvin Thompson	72	Paul Duncan
36	Burnett Magruder	73	Hazel Oblesby
37	Joe Amery	74	Don Frey
38	Walter Sharp	75	John Shank
39	Jim Scott Merritt	76	Larry Dickerson
40	Wiley Thorne	77	Steve Krause
41	Dick Quick	78	Chuck Rainbolt
42	Carl Kenagy	79	Jerry Hill
43	Bob Shornick	80	Jeff Nodell
44	Clayborn Landers		Robba Addison
45	Kermit Whiteaker	81	Brad Gans
46	Bill Nelson	82	Rob Nigh
47	John Truex	83	Mike Smith
48	Bill Overton	84	Mike Smith
49	Tom Bray	85	Karen Edison
50	Bob Shumaker	86	Doug Brasel
51	Bill Bowman	87	David Porter
52	Bill Burkhardt	88	Guy Boyer
53	Ted Harris	89	Craig Zahnd
54	Bill Miller	90	Kelly Skaggs
55	Bill Jackson	91	Eric Zahnd
56	Sam Wallace	92	Jon Booze
57	Jack Armstrong	93	Jenny Buffa
58	Jerry Curnutt	94	Ryan O'Hara
59	Don Herrick	95	Rick Hankins
60	David Burhans	96	Rick Hankins
61	John Brunner	97	Ernesto Herrera-Brito
62	Denny Lambert	98	Quintin Conway

1931 senior class president Everett Webdell supervises appropriate buttoning procedure.

Senate Unbuttons Beanies

For over a century, freshmen survived a fall semester rite of passage known as "buttoning." The Seventeen Rules created by the senior class of 1942, and announced through a formal proclamation, advised that "Each member of this flotsam and jetsam of human degradation shall have procured from the Alumni Office ... a protective head covering in the colors of William Jewell which shall proclaim his or her allegiance to said institution." Freshmen were to wear this beanie at all times on campus until Jewell won its first game, until Homecoming, or until Thanksgiving. (In obeisance to a senior's command they were "to button"— to position the thumb on the button and bend the knees.)

In 1946, with a large veteran presence on campus, the seniors wisely decided not to invoke buttoning. And in 1969, the Senate ended this demeaning activity. (But at least we knew who the other freshmen were.)

Cardinelles and Campus Hosts Serve Campus

In 1968, a small group of women were selected to serve as campus hosts. This program was strongly embraced and shaped by First Lady Virginia Field. In the early years, Cardinelles were trained at the TWA academy for flight attendants in Overland Park.

Since the early 1980s, men have joined their ranks as Campus Hosts, and now fourteen to twenty students are selected each year on the basis of social adeptness, good character, responsiveness, and knowledge of the campus.

They serve as guides and information sources at major college functions including Opening Convocation, Homecoming, Parents Day, Achievement Day, and Graduation. They frequently assist current First Lady Anne Sizemore with the many events at the President's Home.

Re-entry Students Embrace New Horizons

A visit to the New Horizons Lounge in the basement of Gano Chapel reveals the face of the future in higher education: a dramatic increase in re-entry students—those twenty-five and older.

Founded in 1983 by dean of students Johnnie Human as a recruitment tool, support group, and, through its lounge, as a sanctuary, New Horizons has grown significantly over the years.

Membership is open to full-time day students. Though many more re-entry students attend classes at Jewell, particularly in the Evening Division, typically around sixty students meet these criteria.

The New Horizons Lounge is well equipped with a kitchen, computer room, study area, and locker facilities.

STUDENT PUBLICATIONS AND RADIO STATION SPREAD NEWS

Early *Student* Is a *Jewell*

An early student newspaper, the *Jewell*, began publication in the 1870s. The *Student*, which first appeared in 1875, was published by the Excelsior and Philomathic societies. In 1880, it became a monthly paper focusing on literature, science, morals, and general college news. A subscription cost 50 cents per year.

Many will remember the annual April Fools issue of the *Yellow Student* begun in the 1930s.

In 1960, under editor Charles Durbin and advisor Georgia Bowman, the *Student* became a weekly publication focusing primarily on campus news. In 1986, the name was changed to the *Hilltop Monitor* and the publication increasingly embraced off-campus issues

Tatler Yearbook Published

The annual *Tatler* yearbook was first published in 1905 under the leadership of Manley O. Hudson, editor and founder, who later became a teacher, lawyer, and renowned authority on international law.

In 1925 and 1926, the *Tatler* won national recognition with the highest award from the

Members of the 1959-60 journalism class publish weekly Student.

Central Inter-Scholastic Press Association for all class B colleges (300 to 700 enrollment).

From the 1927 *Tatler*: "The *Tatler* is the annual publication of the students of WJC and its purpose is to chronicle the many events of the school year in order that they may endure on the pages of this book and in the memory of the sons and daughters of the Old Hill."

Tatler Revue Draws Crowds

To help finance publication of the *Tatler* yearbook during the Depression, 1932 yearbook editor W. Edward Sharp and business manager Lowell Ditzen, encouraged by Ray Barr, introduced the campus to Tatler Revue. Comprising queen and skit competitions along with a variety of other entertainment, the Tatler Revue was a rousing success. During its zenith, it drew a full house for three

In 1927, Virginia D. Rice won a coveted queen designation.

Candidates for 1970 Tatler Revue Queen: Front row— Daphne Koga, Sandy Payne, Patty Fisher, Pam White, Patty Manzco, Susan Parkmen. Back row— Queen Glenda Knutter, Diane Wilson, Linda Pace, Kay Poppenhagen.

In 1929, Helen Early was selected for one of five queen honors.

evenings, in good part because of the originality, talent, and pushing-the-envelope style of the skits.

Originally, each Greek organization competed independently in the Tatler Revue skits. By the 1960s, sorority-fraternity teams vied for honors along with Non-Affiliated Student Association, Association of Independent Students, and Black Student Association. Criteria were extensive and awards were granted over the years for original music and lyrics, staging, choreography, and staying within the time limits, plus the Ray Barr award for best actor and the Virginia D. Rice award for best actress.

Famous Judges Select Tatler Revue Queens

In 1925, thirty candidates, selected through a student election based on beauty and popularity, competed for five queen designations. From photos of the five, Florenz Ziegfeld, Jr. provided a final ranking. Gary Cooper, Frederic March, and Clive Brook selected the top five queen candidates for 1932.

By the 1970s, competition had evolved to include personality, charm, beauty, poise, talent, and appropriateness of dress. Queen candidates nominated by a sorority, the Non-Affiliated Student Association, the Association of Independent Students, or the Black Student Association modeled both street and formal wear.

By the 1980s, the competition included both a talent segment and a demonstration of social skills.

In the 1990s, a changing perspective on the appropriateness of college women competing in a beauty contest drew the curtain on a long history of Tatler Revue queens.

And now, Tatler Revue has run its course: 1995 was its final year.

KWJC Enlarges Campus Reach

In 1974, William Jewell began broadcasting on FM 91.9 with a ten-watt transmitter. Because the call letters KWJC were in use, the station selected

KWPB (for Walter Pope Binns, former president).

In 1981, the power increased to 240 watts. Programming included a mix of adult contemporary music with contemporary Christian music, news, sports, and a community calendar.

In 1985, the call letters KWJC became available and at the same time the station switched from mono to stereo. As an affiliate of Morningstar, programs are now broadcast twenty-four hours a day.

The station looks forward to becoming a digital multimedia telecommunication service.

In addition to announcing, students enjoy a variety of positions including programming, music, sports, development, production, promotion, and public affairs.

Key faculty members guiding the development of the station have been Dr. Georgia Bowman and Dr. Philip Thompsen. Alumnus volunteer Everett Truex announces many programs. Instructor Kelly Marsh brought new energy and expanded programming to KWJC in 1997.

HOMECOMING ENLIVENS HILL

In many ways, Homecoming is an alumni event–class reunions, an alumni bash sponsored by the board of governors, tailgate parties before the game, and, increasingly, reunions for affinity groups including golfers, lawyers, nurses, athletes, musicians, and Greeks.

But Homecoming has also been a special time

Year	Tatler Revue Queen		
27	Virginia D. Rice, one of 5 queens	66	Penny Kern
29	Helen Early, one of 5 queens	67	Susan Correll
37	Virginia Hessel	68	Lana Jo Farmer
38	Margaret Ruth Lynn	69	Lynda Owen
39	Virginia McNabb	70	Glenda Knutter
40	Madeline Parrott	71	Kay Poppenhagen
41	Audrey Adams	72	Charlene Shepard
42	Lucy Lee Truesdell	73	Lynn Lifritz
43	Ruth Sword	74	Liz Ginn
44	Shirley Vardeman	75	Dee Ann Henry
45	Marilyn Ashley	76	Janet Maag
46	Eunice Todd	77	Lisa Guerrant
47	Jean Beagle	78	Tylie Turner
48	Alice Ann Gallagher	79	Carolyn Crews
49	Judith Borchers	80	JoNel Dayen
50	Beverly McCormick	81	Joey Staton
51	Gwen Moncrief	82	Emily Geilker
52	Jamie Dillmon	83	Diana Nash
53	Donna Radke	84	Lori Greenfield
54	Jean Winkler	85	Beth Dreyer
55	Dorothy Alice Luebeck	86	Lori Andersen
56	Francine Coffey	87	Tammy Mann
57	Pat Cadwallader	88	Luanna Webb
58	Cara Rodenbach	89	Amy Adams
59	Linda Long	90	Roxanne Grant
60	Donna Holmes	91	Elizabeth Bowers
61	Claire Taylor	92	Jenny Lynn Wall
62	Diane Isley	93	Jennifer Opincarne
63	Linda Hanks	94	Hilary Harrington
64	Judy Hall	95	Cynthia Shows
65	Esther Thornton		

for students. Begun during post-Depression years, Homecoming slowly built to all that it encompasses today. In 1933, a parade with floats along with banners and Greek house decorations appeared. By

77

Year	Homecoming Queen		
36	Mary Lynn Pinkerton	67	Mary Fife
37	Margaret Broaddus	68	Sally Adkisson
38	Dorothy Lowry	69	Roberta Keen
39	Beverly Amery	70	Linda Pace
40	Jeanette Ormsby	71	Beth Dunlop
41	Helen Prince	72	Jorine Butterfield
42	Betty Welker	73	Kathi Schirner
43	Penny Paynter	74	Jenna Foster
44	Sally Miller	75	Dawn Webb
45	Clara Jones	76	Linda Rozenbaugh
46	Laura Tapp	77	Dee Ann Henry
47	Polly Quick	78	Robba Addison
48	Jane Bainbridge	79	Kathy Cummings
	& Shirley Landers	80	Karen Isaac
49	Billie Page	81	Dee Dee Jensen
50	Jody Allen	82	Jenny Maynard
51	Judith Borchers	83	Sibby Bruere
52	Joan Sherrill	84	Jodi Jensen
53	Judith Taylor	85	Lori Andersen
54	Sally Sue Boucher	86	Valerie Donnelly
55	Joyce Allmon	87	Stacy Hobelman
56	Francine Coffey	88	Lori Orr
57	Cynthia Hirni	89	Colleen Courtney
58	Sally Lackey	90	Julie Engelhart
59	Kaye Cokely	91	Mary Frazier
60	Claire Taylor	92	Nikki LaBeth
61	Judy Miller	93	Diane Zuo
62	Linda Hanks	94	Lisa Pettijohn
63	Sue James	95	Heather Wiley
64	Sue Ellen Williams	96	Shauna Coffee
65	Marcia Love	97	Jill McCrea
66	Susie Williams		

1934, there were pep speeches and the first victory over Baker in years. The first Homecoming queen was crowned in 1936.

Today, Homecoming is a busy time on the Hill: the Stocksdale Competition Quad Games, Campus Sing, floats and banner contests, Homecoming concert sponsored by the music department, a grand parade through town, an open house at the President's Home, crowning of the Homecoming queen, student open houses for alumni, and, of course, the big game with exciting half-time entertainment.

PERFORMING ARTS FLOURISH

"Jewell Debaters Win Honors"

The above debate headline from the 1960 *Tatler* reflects the outstanding quality of forensics and debate over the years.

The Debating Society was established in 1851. Meetings were held in the college classroom of the original Second Baptist Church of Liberty and every member was required to furnish a candle. In 1881, the Excelsior Society debated the question, "Which exerts the greater influence on the happiness of mankind, the male or female mind?"

In the 1890s, Jewell and Park College set up a debate program traveling between colleges on the train. In 1922, Pi Kappa Delta, the national honorary forensics fraternity, was established, and debate coach P. Caspar Harvey led teams to outstanding national success.

The 1930s saw William Jewell's first direct contact with Oxford University: a tight debate with

After a successful debate trip to California, the 1941 debate team enjoyed the hospitality of film star Eddie Cantor. (from left) Audrey Adams, Madeline Parrott, P. Caspar Harvey, Cantor, and Harry Grassick.

Oxford enjoying a narrow win.

From 1928 through 1930, Jewell produced three consecutive national winners in Pi Kappa Delta competitions: Alden Russell, national extemporaneous title; Lex King Souter, national oratorical title; and Charles Hackler, national extemporaneous title.

In 1947, Georgia Bowman became coach to students from many disciplines who embraced the opportunity to debate under her direction. By 1949, Jewell had won her seventh national first in ten tournaments and covered many miles in a gray Buick to achieve it.

Jewell debaters have remained faithful to this legacy of success. On any given weekend, a van of Jewell students travels to intercollegiate debate tournaments where they compete against an array of colleges and universities. The squad regularly finishes in the Top 100 Sweepstakes ranking of the Cross Examination Debate Association (the national organization for collegiate debate) and has received awards at ten of the last fifteen national tournaments.

Students Embrace Theater

From modest efforts by the literary societies during the late 1800s and early 1900s, theater became firmly established at William Jewell in 1924 with the advent of the J.P. Fruit Dramatics Club, under the sponsorship of John Phelps (Daddy) Fruit. Guided by Virginia D. Rice, whose forty-four-year tenure began in 1930, the William Jewell Players were born.

In 1932, the Beta Pi chapter of Alpha Psi Omega National Honorary Dramatic Fraternity was established on campus with Georgia Bowman as the first president.

Star performers in campus productions whose interest in the arts has continued to impact audiences include the late Marlin (Jim) Davis of

1949 debate team, from left: A. C. MacKinney, Teri Voisey, Norma Ruth Rosendale, Suzie Clark, Joe Taylor, Kenneth Taylor, Wylla Ruth Decker, Judith Borchers, Ella Massey, Georgia Bowman, Dean Lewis, Mary Helen Kennedy, Henry McCanna.

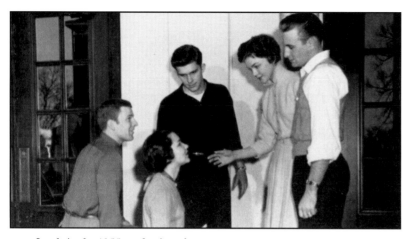

Leads in the 1955 production of Shakespeare's The Winter's Tale, *directed by Virginia D. Rice, include Bill Jackson, Karyl Unruh, Dick Willoughby, Shirlee Wille, and Stewart Carson.*

"Dallas" fame, Richard Harriman as Polonius in *Hamlet*, and Dick Brown as Creon in *Antigone*. Howard Jones, a technical set designer for campus productions, continues as a highly acclaimed creative scene designer.

In 1983, after decades of performing in Gano Chapel, students reveled in the facilities of the new Garnett M. Peters Theater.

Today, student theater performances include an all-campus fall and spring production as well as a senior show that they design and direct, and in which they play a major role. For many senior shows, the audition is open to all students.

Music Program Holds High Note

Music has enriched the Jewell campus from its founding. Today, nearly 40 percent of the student body participates in some form of musical class, ensemble, or private instruction.

Opportunities for instrumental ensembles include the Symphonic Band, the Chamber Orchestra, the Flute Choir, the Jazz Band, the Percussion Ensemble, the Cardinal Brass, and three Handbell Choirs. Vocal music opportunities include the Chamber Singers, Chapel Choir, Concert Choir, and the opera workshop.

A William Jewell orchestra was formed in 1903; the William Jewell Band was performing by 1908, and the Glee Club by 1912. Under the direction of David Grosch, students in the late 1940s and early 1950s produced an elegantly staged series of operas including *Carmen*, *Mignon*, and *Cavalier Rusticana*.

In 1952, the combined men's and women's glee clubs enjoyed their greatest year highlighted with a cast of over one hundred in a repeat performance of the oratorio, *Elijah*, first performed in the '30s.

Ed Lakin's revival of the Marching Band in the 1950s and early '60s ensured enthusiastic band music at each home football game as well as during the Homecoming parade.

1975 Concert Choir in performance under the leadership of Wes Forbis.

Under the leadership of Wes Forbis in the 1960s and '70s, dramatic growth in the music department provided the opportunity for greater student participation in the expanding choral activities. Since the mid-1960s, Don Brown has continued increasing music performance opportunities with Chapel Choir and handbells.

In 1971, the Liberty Symphony began under director Phil Posey. Eighty percent of the musicians, including virtually all the string section of this outstanding group, are William Jewell students, faculty, or alumni.

In 1985, under the direction of Arnold Epley, the Concert Choir began an every-three-years tour of Scotland and England, where the choir has performed in a variety of venues, including many of the great cathedrals, an expansion of the overseas tours introduced by Wes Forbis.

In 1997, the Chamber Orchestra, under the direction of Penny Kruse, was selected by a blind audition tape as the first small college orchestra invited to perform before 3,000 Missouri Music Educators at their annual meeting.

SPECIAL-PURPOSE GROUPS SERVE STUDENTS' NEEDS

AIS/NASA Connect Students

With over half of the student body non-affiliated, the Association of Independent Students (also organized as the Independent Society and the Non-Affiliated Student Association) has played an important, if uneven, role on campus. At times virtually inactive, the organization has periodically enjoyed resurgence as students have sought to participate in Homecoming and Tatler Revue.

In 1948-49, the Independent Society enjoyed a membership of 200 students. The year 1952 saw the society claim many honors: First Lady, Homecoming queen, second place in the Homecoming float, and third in the Tatler Revue skit.

In 1970, the Independent Society took first place with their Tatler Revue skit for the first time in twenty-two years. And in 1978, AIS joined with BSA to take first place in skit competition as well as Queen, Tyler Turner; First Princess and Best Talent, Jane McCrary; and Second Princess, Gwen DeLoach.

From 1985 through 1989, AIS won first place in five consecutive Tatler Revue skit competitions, in part for being the first to use rented backdrops, black lights, and synthesizers.

BSA members Shanice Watson, Fola Akande, and Dr. Cecilia Robinson use Black History Week 1993 to celebrate their heritage.

BSA Serves Special Roles

Begun in 1970-71, the Black Student Association is open to all students on campus. It encourages William Jewell students to work toward harmony in a world of difference.

In the early '70s, Harumba House, the gathering place, was opened in the lower level of Yates College Union. In 1996-97, the Center for Educational Diversity was established in the former Oxford House on East Kansas where it has become a meeting center for BSA as well as for other diversity events. A highlight of BSA history was the 1978 sponsorship of Ralph Abernathy on campus for Black History Week.

Big Sister Council Smoothed Entry

From the 1950s through the mid-'90s, each entering freshman woman was assigned a Big Sister who introduced her to campus, participated in social events with her, and kept in touch during the year. Many strong ties remain from those relationships.

APO Members Serve Campus

The Alpha Mu chapter of Alpha Phi Omega (APO) began as a national honorary fraternity of former Boy Scouts committed to serving campus and community. The Alpha Mu chapter was installed in 1934 by H. Roe Bartle, national APO president, Boy Scout executive, former mayor of Kansas City, and strong supporter of William Jewell. Activities have included serving as flag and banner bearers at all formal convocations, sponsoring a donkey basketball game to help raise money for the new music building, and through the 1980s,

sponsoring the Cutie Pan/Ugly Man (later, Studly Man) competition at Homecoming. Marvin Dixon has served as sponsor of the group since 1966.

Students Benefit from Mentoring

Begun in 1985 by Judy Rychlewski, director of career services, and alumni Mark Bredemeier, Barney Williams, and Sue Heath, the Mentoring program teams students one-on-one with a professional in their chosen field.

Comprising primarily alumni, but including other local professionals, mentors typically meet with their students several times a year, often at the mentor's place of business. This networking opportunity has involved twenty to thirty students per semester with a total of 365 mentees and 303 mentors benefiting from the program.

ADDITIONAL FEATURES ENLIVEN CAMPUS LIFE

Sons of Rest

One early organization, Ye Sons of Rest, has continued to re-emerge over the years. Begun in the 1890s by Dr. John Phelps (Daddy) Fruit, beloved professor of English and philosophy, a small group of senior men claimed a day in the spring to loll on campus and thus formalize their need to slack off. Resting was strictly required in their famous yawn:

> **Raw-buck, Saw Buck**
> **Malum labor est.**
> **Live ever. Work never.**
> **Sons of Rest. Ah-h-h-men.**

One *Tatler* issue enjoyed identifying these campus leaders as *Not honorary, but ornery.*

RAs and RDs Assist in Dorms

Before the 1970s, housemothers and houseparents provided a sense of *in loco parentis* to dorm life, soothing hurts and offering advice. During that era, women students had strict curfews and were required to sign in and out.

Changes have included the employment of resident directors and the use of trained resident assistants prepared to deal with day-to-day student problems. Memorable RDs have included Dr. and Mrs. H.I. Hester, Steve Hemphill, Gary Phelps, Jerry Hill, and David Fulk.

The 1970s and 1980s saw increasing use of off-campus honors houses along with flexibility in permitting upper-class students to live off-campus.

Dining in New Ely an Adventure

Learning the appropriate way to survive the family-style meals at tables of eight in the New Ely Dining Hall meant listening to the sage advice of upper-class students:

1910 Sons of Rest contemplate life.

Try to avoid sitting at tables with jocks ... Although the cooks intend that each person enjoy an adequate meal, receiving the community meat platter after hungry athletes serve themselves may turn you into an unwilling vegetarian ... Remember to dress up for Wednesday night and Sunday noon meals—not only is it required, it also offers an interesting opportunity to see and be seen in your best outfit ... Stay on the good side of the waiter assigned to your table—waiters have power and have devised creative ways to reward or punish you ... Mind your manners; others are noting your sense of etiquette. So, when someone requests the salt, pass the pepper also.

J-Bench Is Endowed Seat

A gift of President Herget in 1929 to honor his graduating class of 1895, the J-Bench was located east of Gano Chapel to provide easy access to customers of the Co-op, then located in the basement of Gano.

Since 1929, the J-Bench has been a popular gathering spot on the Jewell campus.

Students find it a pleasant place to study or visit. Alumni remember earlier days when only athletes wearing letter jackets were permitted to sit there. Later, freshmen wearing their required beanies were denied access. Over the years, the J-Bench has also served as a romantic meeting place.

Now it is fronted by the marble sculpture created by Stanley Boxer, a 1978-79 gift from the students of William Jewell through the College Union Activities Board with assistance from Greg Wirt, project chairman, and the Missouri Arts Council. Spencer Court, given by Helen Foresman Spencer in 1981, shelters both the bench and the sculpture.

Pranks Enliven Campus

In his 1993 Achievement Day address, alumnus Helmar Nielsen recommended embracing a sense of "decent mischief" as one of the value-added liberating arts one gains at a liberal arts institution.

Recollections of such mischief are often reported to the Alumni Office and often remembered with more detail than is merited.

The 1920s: Having honored the five-minute wait for a late professor, the German students began to file out only to discover the professor leaning against the door visiting with a colleague. No problem. The men quietly exited via a first-floor classroom window, gallantly assisting the lone female.

1923: An excited freshman with a new crystal set was testing his antenna, which dangled outside another dorm room. Those occupants attached their antenna to his, hooked up a microphone, and impressed him with his range by providing a German broadcast.

This ruse was so successful they followed it with an SOS call from the Cunard ship, *Aquitania*, complete with breaking waves sloshed in a bucket. However, when the student breathlessly announced that he was calling his father, a Cunard agent, to advise him of the impending tragedy, the wind went out of their sails and they were forced to fess up.

1930: Because guards were posted on Halloween to prevent such pranks, it was a day or two later that Daddy Fruit arrived in his third-floor classroom in Jewell Hall to find that a cow had somehow been assisted up the steps and awaited his lecture.

1946: President Harry S. Truman was the commencement speaker. Upon his arrival, a large contingent of students greeted him. To President Binns' chagrin, many of the men were strikingly decked out with a cane and bow tie. In his address, Truman graciously observed that with an equivalent level of determination and effort directed to the country's problems, they would largely disappear. He returned in 1964 to a more refined welcome.

Early 1950s: Faculty convening their monthly luncheon meeting in the New Ely dining hall were confronted by the powerful odor of steaming limburger cheese. Anticipating their hasty departure into the cold, dining hall waiters had turned off the radiators, smeared the cheese over them, and then turned the radiators back on in the midst of the meeting. Undaunted, the faculty opened windows and continued their meeting.

1953: A heavy sleeper in New Ely was tied securely to his bed, gently lowered out the window, and left to dangle between the second and third floors until he awakened the next morning to the singing of birds and the twittering of amazed passers-by.

1954: When the invited speaker failed to appear for the required chapel service, President Binns chose to read poetry, including his favorite *The Bells* by Edgar Allen Poe. During his reading, a series of hidden alarm clocks began to ring in remarkable synchrony with the repeated refrain "Bells, bells, bells, bells, bells, bells, and bells."

1957: To diminish the quantities of milk carried from the dining hall for late-night snacks, the management cut back on the number of cartons supplied for meals. In protest, students borrowed a horse boarded at the President's Home and led it into the dining hall where it spent the night quartered securely in a corner. Why a horse? "Neither it nor the dining hall gave milk."

1960s: Of course, there were some panty raids, some streaking, and an occasional mooning. One student in the 1960s embraced a financial challenge proffered by members of his dorm by sledding down the front hill on a cafeteria tray minus the protective aid of any clothing.

Late 1970s: In anticipation of Old South week, the Kappa Alpha fraternity mounted an equestrian parade with pride-of-the-South riders delivering invitations to the women's dorms. Uninvited players in the drama, members of Lambda Chi Alpha fraternity dressed as Union soldiers and, led by Abraham Lincoln, met the Southerners in front of Semple Hall and demanded their surrender. Who won? It all depends on whom you ask.

1980s: For many years, the front hill of the campus has been identified by *The Kansas City Star* as one of the five best sledding spots in the city. When Dean Nay, director of the cafeteria for many years, discovered that cafeteria trays were disappearing rapidly on snowy days, he quietly made the old and near-to-being-discarded trays very visible, thus himself contributing to a spirit of decent mischief.

Early 1990s: One morning the faculty received a missive from Panaegis containing amazing grammatical misconstructions and great leaps of questionable logic. Panaegis members were quick to send out a disclaimer. The perpetrators remain at large.

Graduation: Finale and Reunion

May graduation launches seniors into the world and also offers a time for alumni to return, especially those celebrating significant reunion years.

For many years, baccalaureate was held on Sunday at Second Baptist Church while graduation occurred in Gano Chapel on Monday. When the demise of Old Ely provided an open quad, graduation was celebrated out of doors except for those bad or uncertain days that resulted in a last-minute move to Gano and later to the Mabee Center.

During the 1970s, to accommodate family and friends, both baccalaureate and graduation were celebrated on Sunday. And in the early 1980s, the Mabee Center was firmly established as the venue for graduation with a processional contributing dignity and drama to the event. Today, the Caledonian Bagpipe Band and APO flag bearers escort students and faculty in a grand procession around the quad and down the hill to graduation. This is also the day for the pinning ceremony for graduates of the nursing department.

The graduating class, numbering in recent years at around 325, typically contains twenty-five to thirty Evening Division students. The all-time high for graduation occurred in 1989 when 356 students were graduated. As of graduation 1997 slightly over 14,200 students have received a diploma from William Jewell.

Whatever the ceremony, the message is the same: *William Jewell has educated, trained, and guided you for four years. You have worked, struggled, and grown. You are prepared. Now go forth and make us proud. Deo Fisus Labora.*

Graduation on the quad was a glorious event.

CHAPTER 7

CARDINAL ATHLETICS

Cardinal Teams Are Warriors

by Norris Patterson

William Jewell was founded in 1849 as a liberal arts college for men only. In 1917 the first women students were admitted, and in 1921 the college officially became coeducational. During the first fifty years, the enrollment did not exceed 200, and athletics was a voluntary activity–indeed somewhat disorganized until the arrival of President John Priest Greene in 1892.

With the appointment of Dr. Greene, William Jewell entered into an era of curricular change and significant growth in facilities and resources. Of particular interest was the inclusion in 1894 of two years of physical education as a requirement for graduation. In the following year, William Jewell built the first separate building for physical education west of the Mississippi River.

Dr. Greene, with a strong belief in the classical concept of "a strong mind in a strong body," advocated physical fitness as a fundamental part of a liberal arts education. He encouraged sports and games for his all-men's college. It was, perhaps, his earlier study at German universities that influenced the inclusion of physical education in the curriculum,

the construction of a new gymnasium, and the encouragement of team contests.

Organized athletics were not a part of college life until after the Civil War, when there was a national explosion of interest in the various sports that until then had been conducted as "town team" sports. In a general atmosphere of rowdiness, gam-

William Jewell's first baseball team, 1883.

bling, and excessive drinking, the contests often ended in brawls. The post-Civil War college students were interested in athletic competition between colleges, but most college administrators at that time were adamantly opposed to athletic activities on their campuses; in fact, many colleges had rules forbidding such "unintellectual" pursuits.

One man, Y.P. Rothwell, the first director of physical education at William Jewell, was probably the greatest single force in promoting

The baseball team of 1899

Woman's basketball team, 1920

fitness and athletic competition on the campus. He was also the motivating force in building the first gymnasium. A man of vision, Professor Rothwell had studied in the German University of Strasburg and was a pioneer in making physical education an important part of the liberal arts curriculum at Jewell. Rothwell became such a strong force in the state of Missouri that he was hired away from Jewell to be the director of physical education for the newly developing program at the University of Missouri in Columbia. In later years the gymnasium at the University was named in his honor.

The following pages give a chronological listing of some of the important events in the 150 years of athletics at William Jewell College.

1849-1883—There was no organized program of athletics or physical education at the college.

1883—The first organized athletic team appeared on campus in the form of a baseball team arranged entirely by the players themselves. Several games were played against "town teams" or high school teams. After one year, the team was discontinued.

1883-1888—There are no records of any organized athletics on the campus during these five years.

1888—Jewell's first football team was organized by students, led by M.D. Eubank, who was the captain and coach. Very little protective equipment existed, and the students furnished their own uniforms. The first team included thirteen players; the manager of the team was Luther Greene for whom Jewell's football stadium, built in 1955, was named.

Dr. Greene became a prominent doctor in Richmond, Mo., and M.D. Eubank went on to be a medical missionary to China.

1888-1894–There are no records of organized athletics during this period.

1894–Under the leadership of the newly appointed director of physical culture, Younger P. Rothwell, athletics became a college-sponsored activity, and physical education became a requirement for graduation as an important part of the liberal arts curriculum.

1895-1896–Old Brown gymnasium was built at a cost of $12,300. This was the first separate gymnasium building in any college west of the Mississippi.

1896-1898–The college fielded its first college-sponsored football and baseball teams. There was opposition by the faculty to such "ungentlemanly" sports. However, with the support of Y.P. Rothwell and President Greene, both sports were approved by the administration with the stipulation that they be financed entirely by the students.

1898-1899–Jewell fielded teams in football, baseball, and, for the first time, basketball. Player and Coach E.E. Kirkland led the basketball team. Professor Rothwell left Jewell that year to become the director of physical education at the University of Missouri. A noteworthy achievement that year was a football victory over the University of Kansas.

1899-1903–The popularity of football, baseball, and basketball increased each year until financial problems beset the programs. The football team

was forced to cancel the season after two games; basketball continued as the popular sport and highlighted the season with a win over the University of Kansas, whose team was coached by Dr. James Naismith, inventor of the game of basketball.

William Jewell football team, 1899

1903-1904–Financial problems were solved when the students charged an activity fee for athletics which provided funds for better equipment. The students began clamoring for full-time coaches.

1904-1905–The first track team was organized and three tennis courts were built. Track and tennis teams were demanding full recognition and financing as varsity sports supported from student activity funds.

1905-1910–W.O. Hamilton was hired as the first full-time basketball coach. Hamilton later became athletic director at the University of Kansas. Following Hamilton, Alpha Brummage became head coach of all athletics. Under Coach Brummage, Jewell became an athletic power as football went 7-2 and basketball 10-3. Led by Roy Martin, the football, basketball, and track teams excelled. Upon graduation, Roy played football with the "Canton Bulldogs"–the country's first pro team, which became famous with the signing of Jim Thorpe.

1911-1912–Football was again attacked by the

Invitation
to the
Annual Home Coming

William Jewell College
Liberty, Missouri

THURSDAY and FRIDAY
November 1 and 2, 1928

Announcements - Program

faculty as an "ungentlemanly sport that should be abolished." The move to abolish football was led by Professor Charles Durden, a native of Birmingham, England, who sought to substitute soccer for football. The effort failed and soccer was abandoned after only one year.

1912—This was a banner year in athletics as Jewell joined the Missouri Intercollegiate Athletic Association (MIAA) composed of the following colleges: Central College, Drury College, Kirksville Normal, Missouri Valley, Springfield Normal, Tarkio, Westminster, and William Jewell. With the formation of a conference, sports interest reached an all-time high.

1912-1913—R.E. "Dad" Bowles became Jewell's first full-time athletic director. During a career that lasted until 1947, "Dad" coached football, basketball, baseball, track, and tennis. Much of Jewell's long athletic tradition was started and fostered by

"Dad" Bowles. The road that runs through the campus to the football stadium and athletic fields is named for "Dad."

1913-1914—This was another banner year for Jewell athletics in the new athletic conference as the Cardinals won state championships in football, baseball, and track and finished second in basketball.

1914-1918—The next four years were among the best in Jewell's history. The 1915 baseball team was undefeated; the track team began a string of six consecutive championships (Captain "Irish" Farrar set a state record in the 880 at 2.06); tennis teams won state championships four consecutive years; baseball won state championships four consecutive years (A.C. "Mac" McKinney set a national record by striking out twenty-five of twenty-seven batters in a game against Tarkio. Later "Mac" struck out twenty-three batters in a no-hit game against Maryville); and football was either first or second each year.

1917-1918—After the Cardinals won the football championships in the fall, the rest of the sports were canceled as many athletes joined the military in World War I.

1918-1919—With the war's end and the servicemen home, "Dad" Bowles' forces quickly returned to power as they won state championships in basketball, baseball, track, and tennis, and second in football. Myers Mayberry became one of only two five-sport letter winners in Jewell's history, earning letters in football, basketball, baseball, track, and tennis. In addition, he was chosen all-state in football, basketball, and baseball. Probably the most exciting event in 1919 was the arrival of women as full-time students. Shortly thereafter, a women's basketball team was organized that lasted for two years.

1919-1920—State championships were won in baseball and tennis. O.K. "Dimp" Evans became the second athlete to earn five letters in one year. Coincidentally, both Myers Mayberry and "Dimp" Evans were from Farmington, Mo.

1920-1921—As the state colleges (Kirksville, Springfield, Warrensburg, and Maryville) grew to become much larger, the church-related colleges (William Jewell, Missouri Valley, Drury, Tarkio, Westminster, and Central) formed a new conference, the Missouri College Athletic Union (MCAU).

1921-1924—Football and tennis teams were conference champions in 1921. Baseball was dropped from the program. In 1924, as a result of student pressure, baseball was returned on a limited budget, but after two years it was dropped again until 1952.

1924-1925—In the first year in the MCAU, the Cardinals were conference champions in basketball and tennis.

1926-1927—Coach Bill Collins, former Liberty High School coach and Missouri Wesleyan coach, joined the staff to assist "Dad" Bowles, who had coached all sports since 1913.

1927-1928—Bill Collins became head football

Old Brown Gym

and track coach. "Dad" Bowles continued with basketball and tennis. Old Brown Gym was destroyed by fire on January 30, 1928. Construction started on new Brown Gymnasium in April. The students collected $10,000 toward the cost of the new gym.

1928-1929—Marlin Davis, all-conference player and captain of the football team, left school for a movie career under the name Jim Davis, later highlighted by his role as "Jock" Ewing in the TV program "Dallas."

1929-1930—New Brown Gym was dedicated in a game against the University of Missouri; the University of Missouri won 38-22. Golf was added to the sports program for the first time.

New Brown Gym

1930-1934—The tennis championship in 1933 was the only championship during this four-year period. Bill Collins resigned as head football coach and "Dad" Bowles resumed his old position.

1934-1936—It was a sad year as Herman "Polly" Grant died in a swimming accident trying to save a friend from drowning. "Polly" was one of Jewell's greatest all-time athletes. He was all-conference for four years in football and lettered four years in track.

1935-1937—The tennis team won the MCAU championship for the sixth consecutive year in 1937; the 1936 football team won a conference co-championship. In 1937, Jewell fielded one of its greatest track teams as Frank Crane and Coulter Cunningham scored 24 points between them to win the conference meet.

1937-1940—Coach Henri Godfriaux, brother-in-law of "Dad" Bowles and longtime coach at Missouri Valley, became head football coach at Jewell. In his first three years at Jewell, he defeated Missouri Valley 7-6, 7-6, and 6-0.

1941-1945—World War II caused sharp curtailment of Jewell athletics. Navy pre-flight school took over the campus and the athletic program.

1946-1948—The end of World War II brought a great influx of veterans and a return to a full sports program. "Dick" Harp, former University of Kansas star, became head basketball coach, and J.E. "Pat" Bradshaw became head football coach and athletic director. "Dad" Bowles and Coach Godfriaux retired from coaching.

1948-1949—After two successful years, Coach Dick Harp left to become an assistant to "Phog" Allen at the University of Kansas. Harp was replaced by Don Farris, a star football and basketball player of the late '30s.

1950-1951—Rookie coaches Norris Patterson and Jim Nelson came from Danville High School (Ill.) to assume the football and basketball reins. In winning the first football championship in ten years, Jewell broke Missouri Valley's fifty-five game conference winning streak with a 7-6 victory in a game played in the old Kansas City Blues Stadium. Wrestling was added to the Jewell sports program.

1951-1952—After thirty years, baseball was added to the sports program. The football team played in the Corn Bowl in Bloomington, Ill., where they lost to Lewis College 21-12.

1952-1953—Fred Merrell set a NAIA record

(which still stands) with a 55-yard drop kick against Ouichita College. Al Conway was selected as "Little All-American," the leading scorer among all colleges. He gained 1,325 yards in 130 attempts and was the number one choice of the Philadelphia Eagles in the NFL draft.

1953-1954—Jewell won conference championships in football, baseball, and tennis, as baseball became a conference sport. Cross-country was added to the sports program for the first time.

1954-1955—This was a banner year as the Cardinals were MCAU champions in football, basketball, baseball, and track.

1955-1956—A new concrete football stadium was dedicated and named for Dr. Luther Greene, a major contributor and a member of Jewell's first football team of 1888. Norman Short, a star athlete of the 1940s, was named head baseball coach. His team won the MCAU championship in his first year at its helm.

1956-1957—For the first time in history Jewell advanced to the NAIA national men's basketball tournament. This occurred after winning the conference basketball championship and defeating Rockhurst in the district play-offs. Jewell lost in the second round. Coach Norman Short's baseball team, after winning the MCAU championship, earned an invitation to the first NAIA national baseball tournament in Alpine, Texas.

1957-1958—The Cardinal football team beat Hastings College's undefeated football team in the Mineral Water Bowl by a score of 33-14. An interesting sidelight: The captain and quarterback of the Hastings team was Tom Osborne, who became the long-time head coach of the Nebraska Cornhuskers. The basketball team again won the championship but lost to Drury in district play.

1958-1959—Norman Short moved on to become head basketball and baseball coach at the College of Emporia. Darrel Gourley, a successful coach from Chillicothe High School, replaced Coach Short.

1959-1960—This was another winning year as the Cards were conference champions in football, baseball, tennis, and cross-country. The basketball team, after finishing second in the conference, won the district play-offs and went to the final four of the NAIA national tournament. This, without a doubt, was the crowning achievement in Coach Jim Nelson's basketball coaching career.

1960-1961—This period saw championships in football, basketball, and tennis as well as the dedication of the new on-campus baseball field.

1961-1962—Jewell fielded the most successful cross-country team in history, winning the conference and district and finishing fifth in the nationals. The basketball team won the conference and made

Alfred Conway was the leading scorer in the United States with 22 touchdowns and 1,325 yards gained rushing and 379 yards passing.

The 1968 NAIA national baseball champions celebrate.

its third trip to the nationals in an eight-year period. Baseball, golf, and tennis were also MCAU champions. Dr. David Moore, the head of the religion department, coached the first golf championship in Jewell's history.

1962-1963—Fred Flook joined the staff as head coach of baseball and wrestling. Championships were won in tennis, track, football, baseball, cross-country, and wrestling. Clem Buschmann, junior halfback, set an NAIA record as he carried the ball 1,303 yards for an average of ten yards per try. In addition, Buschmann set new conference track records: 9.7 the in 100-yard dash, 21.3 in 220, and 23.3 in the 220-yard hurdles. Bill "PeeWee" Summers set a new high jump record of 6'9 1/2". Swimming became a varsity sport coached by Mary Kinman.

1963-1964—This was another exceptional year as Jewell won championships in football, basketball, baseball, track, golf, and cross-country. Dave Moore's golf team had its greatest year, winning conference and district meets and qualifying for the national meet. Jewell made national history when female Carlene Basore joined the men's tennis team.

Between matches on the men's team, Carlene also won the Missouri Valley women's championship. Bill Summers won All-American honors by jumping 6'9 3/4" to win first in the NAIA national meet.

1964-1965—Conference championships were won in football, basketball, baseball, cross-country, and track. Ray Ritchey, senior kicking specialist, set an NAIA record when he kicked twenty-nine consecutive extra points. His four-year record was forty-nine out of fifty-one tries. Mike Scroggin set a college and conference record in the shot put with a throw of 51'2".

1965-1966—The football team won its fourth consecutive championship. Captain Mike Scroggin received the national scholar athlete award from the National Football Hall of Fame Foundation. Jack Patterson was the first Jewell baseball player selected for the NAIA All-American first team. In addition, he was an all-conference football player and ranked second in the nation with a 48-yard punting average.

1966-1967—Soccer was added to the varsity sports program. Championships included football, basketball, baseball, indoor track, and golf. The baseball team won the district and advanced to the second round of the national meet.

1967-1968—This was also an outstanding year as the baseball team won the national championship, the only national team championship in Jewell's 150-year history. Furthermore, the football team was the first undefeated team in Jewell's history, finishing with a 10-0-1 record, including a tie of

14-14 with Doane College in the Mineral Bowl. That same year saw the end of the coaching career of Norris Patterson. In eighteen years, football teams coached by Patterson and Nelson amassed a record of 131-34-8, including nine championships, three co-championships, and six second-place finishes. Jim Nelson took over as head football coach and John Hickman, former Jewell star and All-American, became head basketball coach.

1968-1969—New head football coach Jim Nelson led the Cardinals to their seventh consecutive football championship. The baseball team won the MCAU championship for the fifth time in six years. They won the district but lost to St. Cloud, Minn., in the area play-offs.

1969-1970—The 1969 football team enjoyed another outstanding year with a 9-1 record, the eighth consecutive MCAU championship, and selection to the Amos Alonzo Stagg Bowl game in Ohio, where the Cardinals lost a close game to the Ohio champion, Wittenberg University. The baseball team won its seventh championship in eight years plus the district and area championships to advance again to the national tournament where they lost in the second round.

1970-1971—For the first time in fifteen years, Jewell failed to win a conference championship in any sport. However, swimming (which was not a conference sport) did enjoy an exceptional year with a 9-2 record. Coach Larry Hamilton's swim team entered the national meet in Clarion, Penn.,

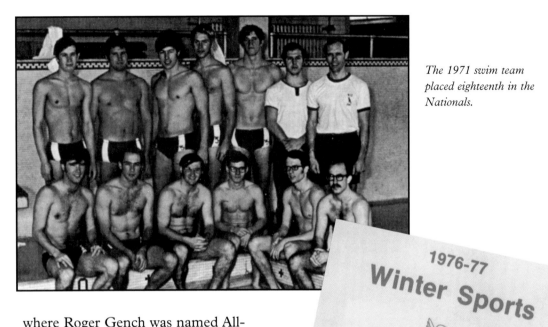

The 1971 swim team placed eighteenth in the Nationals.

where Roger Gench was named All-American by virtue of a fifth-place finish.

1971-1972—After forty-five years the old MCAU conference gave way to a new league—the Heart of America Athletic Conference (HAAC)—composed at the time of William Jewell, Missouri Valley, Central Methodist, Tarkio, Graceland, Baker, Ottawa, and College of Emporia. For the second consecutive year, Jewell failed to win a conference championship. However, the swim team enjoyed a 10-3 record.

1972-1973—This period signaled the arrival of women's sports with full varsity standing. In the first year of women's sports, Jewell fielded teams in volleyball, swimming, basketball, and tennis. There were not yet championship competitions for women's sports in the HAAC. The men's tennis team won the only

95

*Carlene Basore with men's varsity
tennis team which elected her captain*

championship in men's sports.

1973-1974—This was an outstanding year for the Cardinal men as they won the conference all-sports championship plus the sportsmanship trophy; championships in football and baseball; second places in basketball, golf, and tennis; and third in track. The football team was 11-1, including a Mineral Bowl victory over St. Mary's and a loss to Northwest Iowa in the NAIA play-offs. The women's program added field hockey, coached by Barb Macke. Nationally the Association of Intercollegiate Athletics for Women (AIAW) was organized to govern women's athletics. The media were still very slow in publicizing women's sports.

1974-1975—This was a "Cinderella" year for the men's basketball team as they won the Heart of America championship and the district championship to qualify for the NAIA tournament where they lost to Norfolk State in the first round. Women's sports continued to prosper with better equipment, better coaching, and improved budget.

1975-1976—This was another banner year as the men won five championships out of seven sports (basketball, baseball, track, tennis, and cross-country). Coach Fred Flook led the baseball team to a conference, district, and area championship to

qualify for the national meet. The women enjoyed a full schedule in the newly formed AIAW state competition.

1976-1977—Coach Darrel Gourley's teams won the cross-country, indoor track, and outdoor track championships. Coach Fred Flook's baseball team won the conference, district, and area tournament to advance to the national tournament for the second year in a row. The Jewell women participated in state AIAW competition in volleyball, field hockey, basketball, swimming, and tennis, making creditable showings in all sports.

1977-1978—Coach Gourley's track team continued to dominate as they won championships in cross-country and indoor and outdoor track. The cross-country team went on to finish thirty-fifth in the nationals. The baseball team won the championship for the seventh consecutive year. The men's basketball team bounced back to tie for the HAAC title with Graceland. While the women did not win championships, their numbers and quality continued to improve. In addition, the HAAC now sponsored competition in basketball, volleyball, and tennis.

1978-1979—Coach Jim Nelson retired as head football coach and was replaced by Stan McGarvey. Nelson had coached football, basketball, track, and tennis in a twenty-five-year period with great success in all sports. The men's track, cross-country, and baseball teams were again conference champions. The women's program added softball. Women's athletics were making slow-but-sure progress during the 1970s as the men's program grudgingly began to share money and facilities more equitably. While problems at Jewell were minimal, nationally a struggle was getting underway as women sought better opportunities in athletics.

1979-1980—These years saw construction of new baseball, softball, and soccer fields and the near-completion of the new Mabee Center, which made Jewell athletic facilities second-to-none in the Missouri-Kansas area. Championships were won in cross-country and indoor and outdoor track, and the baseball team earned another trip to the national tournament. The crowning performance of the year was Tim Schmid's winning first place in the 10,000 meters at the NAIA national meet in Texas. The women's program added track to its list of varsity sports. Football enjoyed a good year with a 9-1 record and an invitation to the Moila Bowl in St. Joseph, where they lost to Missouri Western.

1980-1981—Men's championships were won in football and baseball. The football team participated in the NAIA play-offs, defeating Baker in the first round and losing to Wilmington College of Ohio in the second round. David Cunningham was chosen first team All-American as he rushed for a record 1,419 yards. The women's basketball team coached by Vic Schultz won the state AIAW championship and advanced to the regionals in Cedar Rapids, Iowa.

1981-1982—This was a notable year as the women's program came alive, winning conference championships in volleyball, softball, and tennis while the men were champions in football, basketball, and baseball. In addition, the women won state championships in basketball, tennis, and softball. Donna Brock set a four-year basketball scoring record of 2,013 points and was selected all-state in both basketball and softball. The football

Greene Stadium, built in 1955 and named for Luther D. Greene

Cardinals, under first-year coach Vic Wallace, were 11-1 as they defeated Pacific Lutheran in the play-offs before losing to Austin College in the semi-finals.

1982-1983—For the eighth time in Coach Flook's twenty years as baseball coach, his team was in the national tournament. Newly appointed Coach Darrel Gourley's team won the men's golf championship (the first for Jewell in the HAAC).

For the second year in a row, the soccer team won the HAAC championship, 1984

Jewell's football team reached its highest achievement as they played for the national championship against Linfield College. After defeating Sul-Ross, Texas, and Northwest Iowa they lost the final game 33-15. Cross-country, coached by Lee Minor, won both men's and women's conference championships.

1983-1984–For the fourth consecutive year, the Jewell football team made the NAIA play-offs, a feat never before accomplished by an NAIA college. They defeated Wilmington College but lost to Northwest Iowa in the second round. "Scoop" Gillespie, four-year starter at Jewell, was drafted by the Pittsburgh Steelers, where he played one year. The men in soccer, cross-country, golf, and track won championships. The women were champions in swimming and cross-country.

1984-1985–Championships in men's sports were soccer, basketball, baseball, and indoor track. The women's track team, led by senior Andrea Eddy, won the conference indoor meet and was second in the outdoor meet. Andrea set seven new school records. Kay Kovar set a new record for women when she lettered in four sports in the same year (softball, volleyball, basketball, and track).

1985-1986–In men's sports, championships were won in football, basketball, track, and base-ball. Incidentally, the Cardinal baseball team defeated both the University of Missouri and the University of Kansas. The Jewell women won championships in cross-country, softball, and indoor and outdoor track.

1986-1987–Championships in men's sports included soccer, basketball (third consecutive year), and baseball (nineteenth time in twenty years under Coach Fred Flook). The women's basketball team won its first championship in the history of the HAAC conference.

1987-1988–After six successful years, Head Football Coach Vic Wallace resigned to accept a position at St. Thomas in St. Paul, Minn.; he was replaced by Stan McGarvey. The basketball team enjoyed a great year winning the HAAC title and defeating Southwest Baptist, Rockhurst, and Drury to advance to the quarterfinals of the nationals, where they lost to Auburn-Montgomery in a very close game. Kim Rivers was selected to be a first team All-American, the first in Jewell's history. The baseball teams were champions for the twentieth time in twenty-one years. The women's basketball team became HAAC champions and their coach Jim Nelson was elected Coach of the Year. The women's cross-country team was again HAAC champions.

1988-1989–Women's basketball and men's golf were the only conference championships achieved this year. The year also marked the retirement of Norris Patterson as department chairman.

1989-1990—The men were champions in cross-country, co-champions in golf, and conference and district champions in tennis; the women were co-champions in basketball. Martha Jordan qualified for the nationals in swimming.

1990-1991—Men's championships were won in football, basketball, and cross-country. Women were champions in basketball. This year saw the introduction of women's soccer coached by Fred Flook.

1991-1992—Jewell men won conference championships in football and basketball while the women won the basketball championship. The men's football team won the district and qualified for the nationals, where they lost in the second round. The men's basketball team went to the quarterfinals in the nationals.

1992-1993—The men's basketball team reached the Final Four of the national tournament in Idaho, where Weldon Stubbs was named to the All-American team. The men's tennis team, under new coach Randall Morris, won the district championship. In men's track competition, Brook Russell broke Clem Buschmann's long-jump record set in 1963.

1993-1994—In terms of win-loss, the 1993-94 year was one of the slimmest in the 100 years of Jewell athletics. The women's cross-country team won the only championship. They won the district and finished twenty-fifth in the nationals. Brook Russell broke Bill Summers' high-jump record by jumping 6'10".

1994-1995—Although the Jewell men's basketball team finished second in the HAAC, they won the conference tournament and a berth in the nationals, where they again reached the Final Four, losing to Bethel (Indiana), the eventual champion. There were no conference championships in 1994-95.

1995-1996—For the third time in four years, the Cardinal men's basketball team advanced to the Final Four of the national tournament. Coach Larry Holley was named the NAIA Coach of the Year and Brook Russell was named NAIA Division II Player of the Year. Russell's honor was greater than that of any other athlete in Jewell history. Because of Russell's remarkable career, the college retired his number, an honor never before conferred on a Jewell athlete.

1996-1997—The men's basketball team won the only championship, which they shared with Evangel. The team went on to finish again in the Final Four of the national meet. Chad Jones was selected to the NAIA All-American squad. Sam Brown resigned as head football coach and was replaced by Jeff Floyd, '79 and a star football and track athlete for Jewell. One of the biggest events of the decade was the building of a new state-of-the-art running track through the generosity of Garnett M. Peters III, a prominent Liberty businessman and longtime supporter of Jewell athletics. Mr. Peters' gift of $250,000 plus contributions by a number of former Jewell athletes made this magnificent facility available for present and future Jewell track events.

Brook Russell was named NAIA Division II Player of the Year in 1996.

WILLIAM JEWELL
COLLEGE

1998
SPRING
SPORTS
SCHEDULE

1997-1998—The men's basketball team, under Coach Larry Holley, again won the conference championship and advanced to the national tournament for the sixth time in seven years. In the past eleven years, Holley's teams have been in the national tournament seven times and have advanced to the Final Four, four times in the past six years.

As the 1998 academic year drew to a close, a major initiative surfaced which promises to have a positive impact on the future of athletics at William Jewell. The board of trustees approved a multi-year plan to upgrade coaching, facilities, and team opportunities for women's sports. Additional funding has been proposed for women's golf, as well as increases in the women's coaching staff, scholarships, operating budgets, facilities, and support staff.

With an ongoing commitment to the development of true scholar-athletes, the winning tradition at William Jewell will continue well into the next century.

FINE ARTS PROGRAM

William Jewell College Far Her Fame Is Known   by D. Dean Dunham, Jr.

*T*here have been many highlights among the hundreds of events presented over more than three decades of the William Jewell College Fine Arts Program. But for the program's founder, Dr. Richard Harriman, one in particular stands out. "Luciano Pavarotti's 1973 recital at William Jewell was an event that almost failed to happen. From the beginning the project faced a series of obstacles. After I had heard him in an operatic performance as Rudolfo in *La Boheme*, I knew I had to bring him to Kansas City for a recital; but I soon discovered that he had no American manager, that there was no one to contact to try to arrange such a performance. It took many months of fruitless inquiry before I finally made contact in 1971 with Herbert Breslin, then his public relations representative, later to become his manager. Herbert agreed to try to persuade Luciano to prepare a recital program, but then the next obstacle arose: the fee. Herbert named a figure for this new, unknown singer that was greater than the fees charged by the most famous tenors of that time. 'But no one has ever heard of Luciano Pavarotti,' I protested. I still

recall Herbert's reply, which was pointed and very memorable. 'They will,' he said.

"I knew he was right. I agreed to the fee, and the contracts were signed. In the intervening year and a half, articles about the new tenor began to appear in major magazines, records became available, and his spectacular singing in *The Daughter of the Regiment* at the Metropolitan Opera attracted national attention. When the week of the recital arrived, I was eager and excited about this exceptional event.

"The recital was to be Thursday, February 1, and Luciano was to fly to Kansas City on Tuesday afternoon. Tuesday morning I received a call from Herbert, 'I don't know if Luciano will be able to perform on Thursday,' he said. 'He has a terrible cold and can't sing at all now. He had to cancel the

Luciano Pavarotti

Midori

Cecilia Bartoli

Metropolitan last night. He won't be flying to Kansas City today.' "

Pavarotti did arrive on Wednesday and did recover by Thursday. The story from there is familiar: He sang on the Gano Chapel stage; He kept a large white handkerchief in his left hand throughout the evening, and the William Jewell audience that night saw Luciano Pavarotti's trademark symbol in use for the first time. "The recital was glorious, the audience was ecstatic ... at the time I thought we had heard his first American recital; it wasn't until later that I learned it was his first professional recital anywhere," Harriman said.

Herbert Breslin was correct; audiences did hear of him. And it was a proud and significant moment for Richard Harriman, the man who had the remarkably developed taste and prescience to persevere in bringing Luciano Pavarotti to the William Jewell campus. In fact, he brought the great tenor to the William Jewell College Fine Arts series four more times. That same taste and

inflexible insistence on presenting only the best have created many other American professional recital debuts on the William Jewell program: violinist Maxim Vengerov and vocalists June Anderson, Ileana Cotrubas, Luciana Serra, Carol Vaness, Thomas Allen, Francisco Araiza, Sergei Leiferkus, and Yevgeny Nesterenko. Cecilia Bartoli also counts William Jewell as the program on which she gave her professional recital debut here in the United States.

The story of the William Jewell College Fine Arts Program is the story of Richard Harriman's more than thirty-five years of contribution to the arts education of William Jewell students and to the arts experience of generations of Kansas City audiences. It is at heart the story of his remarkably developed taste and his dedication to excellence.

William Jewell students who took classes with him as their classmate in the early '50s and who took classes from him as their English teacher are not astonished by his remarkable knowledge of the theater arts. Nor are his teachers, Virginia D. Rice '28 and Georgia B. Bowman '34. He was a comic actor of disarming finesse, an oral interpreter of expressive range and thoughtful depth, and a teacher of great effectiveness and popularity. Former students remember his Shakespeare classes with clarity and fondness. They respected his authority and understanding of drama based on his study, his professional education, and his interpretive and pedagogical talents. Trips to New York and

London theaters several times each year put him in the audience for first productions of the plays of Eugene O'Neill, Arthur Miller, Tennessee Williams, John Osborne, Harold Pinter, Tom Stoppard, Edward Albee, and August Wilson, among others. Students always knew they were in the presence of one who had studied deeply the works by and the criticism of Shakespeare, and who had seen all thirty-seven of the Bard's plays in professional production, most of them many times over. He was a witness; he professed the importance of the arts.

And his knowledge of plays, dramatic traditions, and the theater has informed the Fine Arts Program over its years, even though traveling theater companies are now almost a feature of the past. Richard Harriman has presented the New York-based Acting Company a dozen or more times since 1975; the Guthrie Theatre five times during its touring phase; and the Royal Shakespeare Company, the Young Vic Company, and the National Theatre of Great Britain many times while they toured. William Jewell students saw their first professionally acted Shakespeare, their first Ibsen, their first George Bernard Shaw, and their first Mamet on the series; for Kansas City audiences many of these same plays had not been available before the Fine Arts Program brought them. Theirs was the opportunity to hear Tom Stoppard, Edward Albee, Athol Fugard, Arthur Miller, and Arthur Kopit speak in person about their art. It was also theirs to see performances by Claire

Arthur Miller

Bloom, Julie Harris, Celeste Holm, Sir Michael Redgrave, James Whitmore, and others.

Even his high school friends would not be astonished to know the results of Richard Harriman's lifetime of experience in the musical arts. A group of his teenage classmates and he made it a common source of pleasure to attend presenters' series in Kansas City: the Town Hall and the Ruth Seufert series. They were in the audience for many soloists and groups and for the presentations of ballet companies. Harriman continued to pursue his love of music and dance on those trips to New York, London, and the Continent, mixing theater events with operas, recitals, concerts, and ballet performances on most trips. When he served in the U.S. Army after graduating from Jewell, he was stationed in Washington, D.C., and made weekend trips to New York. In graduate school at Stanford University, he frequented arts events in San Francisco and other West Coast venues. He started early, taken to events as a child and youth by his parents, and has continued on his own throughout his life.

James Galway

Jessye Norman

Sir Michael Redgrave

And again, it is an experienced and informed taste that shapes the high quality of the Fine Arts Program's history and tradition of bringing vocalists, pianists, violinists, and other instrumentalists, chamber groups, and world-standard-setting orchestras to Jewell students and area audiences.

The list is remarkably long, especially when one considers the repeat performances of many artists: more than four dozen pianists, including widely recognized names such as Jose Iturbi, Emanuel Ax, Philippe Entremont, Alicia de Larrocha, Rudolf Serkin, and Andre Watts; more than a half-dozen cellists, including Yo-Yo Ma and Mstislav Rostropovich; two-dozen-plus violinists, including Yehudi Menuhin, Midori, Itzhak Perlman, and Isaac Stern; a good handful of great flutists, including James Galway, Jean-Pierre Rampal, and Paula Robison; harpists; organists, and guitarists, including Nancy Allen, Virgil Fox, Carlos Montoya, and Andres Segovia; and the Academy of St. Martin-in-the-Fields, the Royal Philharmonic, and the Philadelphia Orchestra.

The list of important artists also includes the mezzo-soprano Cecilia Bartoli, who was 23-years-old and still a "rising young star" when she was scheduled for her American recital debut on the Jewell series. Her appearance on the program is illustrative of another feature of Richard Harriman's leadership. He was, and remains, determined that the Fine Arts Programs serve the educational purposes of William Jewell students. In fact, not well known to many concertgoers is the Education Series, which often parallels live performances. This series brings master classes to the Jewell campus. Such opportunities—sometimes six or seven in a year—have been exciting and valuable to student performers and their teachers; they are the envy of many music students throughout the metropolitan area. Because of his educational commitment, Harriman has always been open to scheduling artists just beginning their careers; indeed, his contacts in musical management organizations have known that he wants to present debuts, in the tradition begun with the Pavarotti recital and continuing with that of Cecilia Bartoli.

To maintain a high caliber of programming, he has had to continually increase his knowledge, just as in a scholarly discipline one has to "keep up." Reading *The New York Times* and *Opera News* is but a small part of his dedicated reading. He also listens to recordings and, of course, attends performances. He first noted Bartoli in a *Grammophone* review of her first compact disc, not then available in the United States. Soon after, her management sent him a promotional tape, knowing of his possible interest in scheduling her. Because of his discernment, Harriman did sign her and presented her in the 1990-91 program, another coup for William Jewell students and the Kansas City audience. It was just one more instance of his experience and knowledge in action.

The potential disadvantage of his consistent achievement is that he will be taken for granted by the audiences who benefit by his leadership. However, in a spirit of service, Richard Harriman is not troubled by that risk. He lets the program speak for itself.

Because of the program's virtues, William Jewell College is well known to musicians across the Western world. Leontyne Price loved singing in Gano Chapel for its complimenting acoustics and was on the series five times. Marilyn Horne made the program an important part of nine of her tours, and she has since included the Jewell series in her sponsorship of young artists. Martin Katz, one of the very few at the top of the list of in-demand collaborating pianists, knows well Richard Harriman, the music faculty at Jewell, and some of the college's students, so often has he been on the program and made himself available to give master classes. Phillip Glass lectured in Peters Theater on campus. The members of the St. Louis Symphony Orchestra, Leonard Slatkin, and his successor frequently include Jewell in their season. The choirs

Vengerov

Marilyn Horne

of English cathedrals and of Oxford colleges and the David Parsons Dance Company know William Jewell, its student audiences, and its Kansas City patrons, subscribers, and participants.

The college, the program, and Richard Harriman are also well known by arts business agents, agencies, management, and promoters. The business sense with which Harriman began the program was clearly adept and savvy. Always quiet, generally reserved, always courteous, always well informed, he has always been firm in insisting on high quality, the best. He negotiated with Sol Hurok management, with Columbia Artists, with ICM, and with Shaw. He worked out of gumption and self-assurance right from the start; for example, to associate with one agency would have been an easy way to begin a series, but it would provide a platform for only that agency's artists. He says the temptation "never

105

Paul Taylor Dance Co.

occurred to me." Instead he chose to select each artist and each year's program one by one. According to Harriman, "I know which artists I want. I look at available lists. I weigh the offers on phone contacts from management, with many of which I've never done business."

As an English teacher who began the Fine Arts Program out of educational ideals, he showed extraordinary business capabilities. The beginning, appropriately enough, took place in Jewell Hall, in a tiny two-teacher office and during one of those conversations that took the measure of the distance between perceived reality and arching ideals.

Harriman and Dean Dunham elaborated their hopes into a proposal to the college administration; President H. Guy Moore caught the spirit of the dream and moved to support it.

The William Jewell College Fine Arts Program has become a Kansas City institution. It is accompanied and supported by a Fine Arts Guild, a Society of Patrons, and a Second Generation organization. The business and social leaders of Kansas City and its region recognize William Jewell most of all through this program; those leaders choose to come to Fine Arts events, then to support the program, and then to recognize William

Jewell's powerful impact on the community. It is not lost on them that Richard Harriman is a leader with whom they enjoy associating, and many well-connected audience members have become personal acquaintances or close friends. Their lives have been directly affected by what he and the William Jewell College Fine Arts Program have brought them.

The judgment with which Richard Harriman has guided the experiences of so many, whether they be initiates or themselves thoroughly seasoned, is the expression of a lifetime of learning and of a unique persona. It is a powerfully influencing sensibility that has made and continues to make an important impact.

Those in the William Jewell community who know Richard as a friend, colleague, teacher, and mentor know him as one who has shaped their William Jewell experience. He gives much credit to his many staff members, including Charlotte Apple, Janet Hill, Kathy Dunn, Anna Roberts Buckner, Carol Croley, and Clark Morris. All acknowledge that they have been strongly affected, shaped, and educated by his leadership. Many students have had striking and significant realizations about the power of the arts and about the power of human expression. Many have learned profound human meanings. Many have learned about themselves and have been reinforced in following their own talents and, whether artists themselves or not, have nurtured their own possibilities.

And after all, the history of the William Jewell College Fine Arts Program, in its more than three decades of presenting fifteen, eighteen, twenty events each year, has been the history of successive individual persons having powerful moments—some of them peak lifetime experiences—of illumination and even intense joy. They remember specific events that made a difference in their lives. The Fine Arts Program is a monumental legacy.

Kiri Te Kanawa

Itzhak Perlman

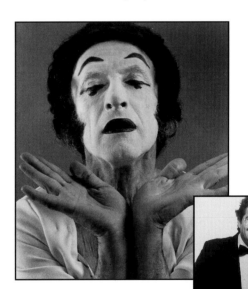

Marcel Marceau

Emanuel Ax & Yo Yo Ma

107

Richard Harriman

POSTSCRIPT

By Richard Harriman

Reading Dean Dunham's chapter about the Fine Arts Program reminds me what a kind person he is. His description of the program is very generous to me, but very modest about his own contributions. The record should show that it was Dean's idea to create such a program at William Jewell College.

Because I shared an English department office with him in Jewell Hall, I became involved in the project. We both worked hard to get the program established, but I believe the greater effort was his. The document that articulated the vision of the program was signed by both of us, but was composed by Dean.

President Moore's decision to create the Fine Arts Program coincided with Dean's decision to leave the college temporarily to do further graduate work. As a result I was appointed director of the Fine Arts Program, and since then my life has never been the same. When Dean returned to the faculty four years later, he became my greatest source of support and inspiration. His usual seat at the Folly Theater is directly behind mine, a pleasant reminder that the co-founder is always behind me, lending his counsel and encouragement. He rejoices with me in the program's successes and pretends not to notice the failures. I could not ask for a better colleague and friend.

American Ballet Theatre

Bolshoi Ballet

CHAPTER 9

WOMEN AT WILLIAM JEWELL

Bold and Brave and True

by Georgia Bowman

*A*lthough the *Catalogue* statement had been terse and minimal, the announcement of the admission of women to William Jewell created ebullience in the September, 1917, issue of the *Student*. Read the 30-point headline:

GIRLS! GIRLS! GIRLS!
Our Time Has Come At Last and They
Are Now About the Hill

Actually, the ten young women who first enrolled were not really on or of the Hill yet. They were assigned to an off-campus classroom known as the Annex, under the chaperonage of a "Mrs. Swinney." Classes were held in that location, but the girls of necessity often climbed the hill for library and laboratory work and to attend their personal ethics class taught by the college president, Dr. John Priest Greene.

The "girls" quickly launched into campus activities—the newspaper staff and a basketball team. The trustees remained ambivalent. The 1919 *Catalogue* read:

The trustees of the college have again decided to admit young women to the Collegiate Department without fully committing the institution to coeducation.

By the next year they had backed away from the whole idea, deciding to permit only those already enrolled to continue, but admitting no others.

The *Student* continued its enthusiastic support for coeducation; however, it noted that by 1919 the women's scholastic average was 96.07, that of the men was 85.60. So women stayed, and the college gradually undertook efforts to provide an official dormitory. Melrose Hall was financed by an anonymous donor and built at a cost of $75,000.

First ten "Jewells" on the Hill

109

Mrs. Leona Kresse–the first woman to graduate from William Jewell, 1920

None of the first ten coeds was the first woman to be graduated. That distinction went to Mrs. Leona Kresse '20. Mrs. Kresse had earned credits at Central Missouri State Teachers College (now Central Missouri State University), and with her ministerial student husband enrolled with advance standing. Keeping house, heading the new Coeds Club, playing basketball, studying, and caring for the couple's small daughter were new challenges. In addition, Mrs. Kresse was the first woman student assistant. As a senior she also taught a class in freshman algebra.

Her connection with the college remained close. After graduation, as a teacher at Hardin High School, she encouraged a prize pupil, Wallace Hilton, who became nationally known in his work as head of the William Jewell physics department. Moreover, in 1933 Mrs. Kresse brought her daughter, Estelle Anna, to enroll in the college. In the mid-'90s, the title of the senior honored as First

Lady of the campus was changed to honor the memory of Mrs. Kresse.

As the years passed, women took places in every area of campus life. Beauty reigned in 1924 when the Tatler Revue showcased not one but five queens. Brains as well as beauty flourished with Mary Margaret Jesse as the first woman editor of the *Student* and four other women, including her sister Ruth, on the staff. By 1926, six women were on the debate squad.

Two sororities appeared in the '20s: Iota Pi– 1919 (later moving into national Beta Sigma Omicron, which in turn merged in 1964 with Zeta Tau Alpha) and TNT (1922), which went national as Alpha Delta Pi in 1949. Alpha Gamma Delta arrived in 1946, and Delta Zeta in 1961.

Soon other women's organizations sprang up: Sigma Rho, YWA, Beta Lambda, and Panaegis. Sigma Rho's first eleven members included young women who were preparing for church or mission work. The Young Women's Association, a branch of the Southern Baptist Convention's Young Women's Association, had the dual purpose of mission study and social activities. Beta Lambda, a female biology society, later merged with the larger Beta Beta Beta.

Enduring the longest among these was Panaegis. Created in 1928 by Professor P. Caspar Harvey, it was for half a century the most prestigious honor society on campus. Limited to seven senior women, its aim was to elevate the status of women and provide service to the college. Much of these same purposes continue since Panaegis was received as the Panaegis Chapter of Mortar Board in 1978. Nationwide, women lost their singularity in this honor group when government regulations dictated that Mortar Board must admit men.

The Great Depression curtailed the college in many ways. Buildings went unrepaired, faculty salaries were cut, and student help at 20 cents an hour performed most campus services. Through the diligence of President John F. Herget, the college survived. So did women students, although their social life was strictly circumscribed by the regulations of Melrose Hall. The printed booklet of Melrose regulations in the early '30s read thus:

Social functions on Sunday are to be avoided in such a way as to make the day one of quiet dignity and worship. It is expected that all girls attend religious services sometime during the day.

Monday, Tuesday, Wednesday and Thursday are study nights. There will be no dating nor social functions in Melrose on these nights.

During the months of September and October, April and May, girls are privileged to walk after dinner, provided they are in Melrose by study hour—7:30 p.m.

Girls are not permitted to leave town, go to nearby towns or cities for the day or part of the day, or go out for meals, without permission.

Girls have the privilege of going home any weekend, provided permission is granted by the supervisor.

Girls may receive callers on Friday and Saturday evenings 7:30-9:50 p.m., on the night before any college holiday, and on completion of their examinations.

Even the residence in Melrose Hall of President Herget's niece, Margaret Long, did not mitigate the rigidity of those rules, which were a bone of female contention for years. From their first arrival on campus, women had been relegated for their studies to the glass-tile-floored balcony of the library, and they learned biology in girls-only classes with a woman teacher.

Women joined the faculty ranks in the '20s and '30s. First was Mary Elmore, assistant to her professor father, Dr. J.C. Elmore, chairman of the biology department. Next came Eleanor Burton, employed to teach those segregated women's biology classes. Arriving fresh from a master's degree at the University of Kansas, Virginia D. Rice assumed not only a full courseload in the English department, but also developed Jewell's first and ongoing theater program. Perhaps not insignificantly, her first production was Ibsen's *A Doll's House*, which dealt with the theme of women's emancipation. Miss Rice bears the honor of teaching longevity among women faculty members: 46 years. Georgia

Mary Elmore– the first woman faculty member, 1928

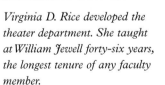

Virginia D. Rice developed the theater department. She taught at William Jewell forty-six years, the longest tenure of any faculty member.

William Jewell women who served in World War II	
Jeanne Anderson, SPAR	*Florence Knicke, Army nurse*
Elizabeth E. Berge, WAC	*Mary E. Kugler, WAVE*
Annajane Burkhardt, WAVE	*Jane Quick, WAVE*
Kate Byrd, WAVE	*Marie M. Tipton, Army nurse*
Wilellen Capps, WAVE	*Ann Tripp, WAC*
Rada Mae Corrigan, WAVE	*Ramona Tripp, WAC*
Lillian Marie Crenshaw, Army nurse	*Nellie Turner, WAC*
Mildred Gash, WAVE	*Helen VanDyke, WAC*
Maxine Hattaway, WAVE	*Martha A. Morgan Walby, WAC*
Ruth E. Hayes, WAC	*Martha Witthaus, WAVE*
Martha Hoover, WAVE	*LaVerne York, service not listed*

Because of the turmoil of the times, an accurate record of women who actually went to war is probably incomplete, but this list is compiled from reports in the college Alumni Bulletin.

Bowman, communication, and Olive Thomas, biology, held forth with 40 1/2 and 38 years, respectively.

During the thirties, student publications showed an ever-increasing number of women in responsible roles: *Tatler* editors were Lucille Hall (Chiles) and Nelda Green; the *Student* staff list read like the membership of the two sororities. Debate circles were equally invaded. Pi Kappa Delta, the national forensics society, had a membership of six women and nine men. Mary Belle Burch and Georgia Bowman teamed to win a state debate championship. Both later taught at the college. Mary Belle and teammate Grace Prewitt, under forensics director P. Caspar Harvey, traveled coast to coast on the longest trip ever taken by a women's team. A few years later, Audri Adams and

Madeline Parrott made an 11,000-mile trip through thirteen states, achieving distinguished records in both debate and individual events.

When he was director of public relations, Professor Harvey often declared that "Any 'First' is good publicity." By the time of World War II there were few campus "Firsts" to be gained by women students. In the absence of men gone to war, however, women dominated almost every facet of campus life. In fact, Shirley Conkling and Juanita Edmondson wanted to be ready to fight if necessary and enrolled in a program to learn to fly sponsored by the Civil Aeronautics Association. Others sold war bonds and contributed to the Red Cross.

Among the women not in direct military but in allied services were Eunice Wagner and Mildred Mason (later administrative assistant to Senator Henry Jackson), Red Cross; Dorothy Phillips, recreational director, Army Air Force; Mildred Stoeltzing, civilian engineering aide in airborne radio at Wright Field, Dayton; and Dorothy Woods, civilian department head for visual aids at the U.S. Command and General Staff College, Leavenworth.

As the war widened, the ranks of male faculty and students thinned. However, administrative planning provided some compensation for the loss of male students. The Navy awarded the college a contract for a Naval Flight Preparatory School.

Contingents of cadets moved in and out for three months of preflight training. These men were quartered in Melrose Hall, so the girls were moved into the nearly empty fraternity houses, and the remaining fraternity men were housed in New Ely. The President's Home became Colonial House; Sigma Nu House, Hilltop House; K.A. House, Arlington Hall; and Phi Gamma Delta House, Harmony Hall. The last cadets left in 1945, and campus life began to return to normal.

With peacetime, a new dean of women appeared: Miss Alma Hunt, who after her years at Jewell became internationally known in Baptist circles as executive secretary of the Women's Missionary Union of the Southern Baptist Convention. In 1958 she was awarded an honorary degree of humanities by the college.

The next dean of women, Miss Catherine Bates, faced the perennial complaint about women's hours with at least a partial solution. In late 1950 the good news was that juniors and seniors would have midnight privileges Friday and Saturday nights, and men would be allowed to visit in the Melrose lounge each evening. (The general reaction was "Big deal!–Huh!")

Some young women are leaders as undergraduates; others become leaders as they enter professions. One of these was Frances Lindsay. Who but a mathematics teacher could budget a $75-a-month salary so as to make a monthly contribution to her alma mater? When in mid-Depression Dr. Herget wrote a letter to alumni asking them to contribute one dollar a month, Frances Lindsay responded, and had a record of contributions—much more than

a dollar a month—every year from the time of her first teaching job until shortly before her death.

Dorothy Truex was never a shy little violet. Active as an undergraduate, she earned an M.A. from the University of Missouri Columbia, a Ph.D. from Columbia University, and a professional Diploma of Dean of Women. As a dean she worked at both the University of Oklahoma and the University of Arkansas, Little Rock. In a busy schedule she also found time to serve as the first woman president of the William Jewell Alumni Association, 1971-1973.

In the post-war years the *Student* noted variously that Carrie E. Sprague had become a doctor in Binghamton, N.Y.; that Lucy Herget, daughter of President Herget, was elected to Panaegis and *Who's Who in American Colleges and Universities*. She later became a businesswoman in Cincinnati. Mary Louise and Elizabeth Derwacter, daughters of Registrar F.M. Derwacter, left their permanent mark on the college as successive editors of the *Tatler*. The 1948-49 centennial edition by Elizabeth won an All-American rating. Paivi Ahonen came from Finland so fluent in English she was selected co-editor of the *Student* her sophomore year. She returned to Finland, earned an advanced degree, and became a high school English teacher.

A name appearing often in the campus newspaper was that of pretty little Myra Lane: Sigma Tau Delta secretary, winner of poetry awards, president of Alpha Gamma Delta and Panhellenic, forensics

*First members of
Panaegis, 1928*

squad, English assistant, *Who's Who*, Panaegis, lead in the senior play. Armed with an M.A. and a Ph.D., Myra Lane Unger returned to the college and retired in 1996 after thirty-six years of teaching in the English department with emphasis on women's studies.

The name of a student who works twenty hours a week as a telephone operator and more hours as a psychology assistant does not appear often in the social items of a campus paper. So it was with Dr. Neita Frohmuth. She starred academically, however: Dean's List for four years, Phi Epsilon, M.A. from Harvard, and Ph.D. from the University of Missouri, Kansas City. Neita Frohmuth Geilker, wife of physics department chairman Dr. Don Geilker, has her own enterprise in business communication. She has remained closely associated with the college as an officer of the Woman's

Committee and from time to time a teacher in the English department.

In yet another field, Mary Jo Smith, biology major, debater, and a queen of the American Royal, found that a doctorate from the University of Tennessee and co-authorship of numerous scientific studies have led to a rewarding career in cancer research.

The law is well represented by Linda French. After a busy four undergraduate years she graduated from law school, served as vice president and general counsel for Payless Cashways, then moved to the faculty of William Jewell. As a volunteer for the Red Cross, she is now an honorary life member of that service organization.

Departments that emphasize activities and performance have produced a series of outstanding graduates. From the department of music came Rosemary Harrell Jackson. Both actress and vocalist, she sang in the Starlight Theatre chorus in Kansas City. This was a forerunner to a successful professional career including teaching at Drury College. Another music major was Suzanne Wolfe. Singing professionally in Milan, Italy, she married and chose to continue her career there. Cindy Shepherd, or with proper dignity, Dr. Cynthia Shepherd, became professor of music at Howard Payne University. Not to be confused with her is Charleen Shepard, who has continued to charm with her lovely voice as she teaches at Friends University.

Both men and women instructors have helped develop the talents of students in every department. In the music department, Dr. Pauline Riddle has been a role model for more than twenty-five years. As director of keyboard studies, she wrote four full-length organ study books as well as a series for the keyboard magazine of the Southern Baptist Convention. She has been vice president of the Educational Division of the Southern Baptist Music Conference and dean of the Kansas City chapter of the America Guild of Organists.

Starting as a modest effort in 1970, the nursing department has grown from ten students and two instructors to a department that in the mid-'90s had graduated 584 (nineteen men) state-qualified nurses. Under the leadership of Dr. Jeanne Johnson, twenty-four years on the staff, the fully accredited department has a remarkably high percentage–90 to 100 percent–of success in student certification by the state nursing board. This fact, along with demanding instruction by such teachers as Dr. Ruth Edwards, has made William Jewell nurses popular with area hospitals. A long list of significant honors marks Dr. Edwards as an outstanding educator.

Women are often charged with talking too much. The department of communication has produced women speakers who are logical, organized, and professionally competent. Trophies in both women's and open competition have come to orators and debaters like Ruth Ellen Halter, Mary

"Little Women" Drama

Helen Kennedy, and Linda Ehrsam and from debate teams like Rose Ellen Clark and Wylla Ruth Decker; Joyce Parr and Mary Jo Smith; Anita McPike and Norma Ruth Rosendale; Aloah Burke and Ann Faubion; Georgia Pearson and Cindy Hoover; and Linda Hopkins and Stephanie Teeter.

As Title IX took effect, more opportunities for women opened in athletics. Leading the way was Carlene Basore, first woman member of the J Club. A state high school tennis champion, she was the Missouri Valley Collegiate champion. Her playing in the NAIA men's divisions brought male protests, but she played and won nevertheless, and made the Dean's List all four years, besides. Another star, a swimmer, soon arrived. Christie Freeman won awards in France, England, and Australia, and the women's water ski slalom in France. Well into the '90s another woman made the J Club, Donna

William Jewell women who served as foreign and home missionaries

Doris Jean Gibson Bellington	*Miriam Lou Misner*
Lisa Bohannon	*Shirley Ann Nowlin Peach*
Mildred Ruth Steckler Brown	*Barbara Dee Warren Peterson*
Mary Ruth Carney	*Wanda Lyvonne Ponder*
Bonnie Troop Costa	*Amy Jo Perdew Purl*
Ona Belle Cox	*Mary Jones Quick*
Beverly June Stephens Curp	*Patricia Reed*
Heather Duncan	*Nona Tremain Renfrow*
Elma Elam	*Marcia Lynne Jones Richardson*
Marie Sadler Eudaly	*Dorris Ann Fuson Robinson*
Doris Hauk Fowler	*Wanda Mae Beckham Schweer*
Marjorie Royston Fuller	*Darlyne Horner Sears*
Janet Harvey Graves	*June Tinsley Seat*
Shirley Kay Butler Harner	*Jessie Settle*
Eunice Listrom Harvey	*Helen Mitchell Sherer*
Ruth Everley Hayes	*Linda Susan Shrimpton Springate*
Alice June Leavitt Hurst	*Shea Strassberger*
Barbara Ramona Smith Hurst	*Leona Marie Walker Troop*
Elizabeth Ruth Qualls Justl	*Diana Sue Wolfe Wade*
Katya Karathanas	*Thelma Edna Williams*
Marian Louise Kammler Leftwich	*Glenda Ruth Burk Wolfe*
Vickie Tapp Malott	*Sheryl Woods*
Helen Iola McClellan Manoogian	*Charlotte Worley*

Brock. She won awards in swimming, but her greater interest was in basketball, where she was a team mainstay for her entire college career.

From the department of religion have come scores of women missionaries, ministers, and church-related workers. Ordained ministers include Connie Andress Stinson, Patricia Stuart Jacobs, Marty Matthews Barr, Jo Ellen Witt; Dr. Judith Craig (one of three women bishops of the United Methodist Church) Ruth Ann Stark Smith and Betty June Winston Smith (Christian Church), and Betty Stone, (Congregational Church).

Employed to teach, and unencumbered by administrative demands to publish or perish, women faculty members have achieved significance in their fields at local and national levels.

Dr. Judith Dilts, chair of the biology department, received three college honors in a single year: Advisor of the Year, the Faculty Development Award, and the Carl F. Willard Distinguished Teaching Award. These were but the culmination of a long list of grants, honors, and accomplishments in previous years. During two sabbaticals her specialized studies centered on neurobiology and molecular biology. At the college she has computerized the biology department and developed a program of undergraduate research. With National Science Foundation grants and the Northland Excellence in Teaching Award, she has still found time to look out into her community. She instigated and organized the popular Liberty Recycling Program.

Three Humanities Council grants, three faculty papers, scholar lecturer for the American Speakers' Bureau, eight campus literary programs featuring African-American writers, youth leadership workshop on "Preparing to Lead in a Multi-Cultural World"–these are but a few of the activities of Dr. Cecelia Robinson, English professor. She also has developed a major project, the Pens Across the Metroplex Pen Pal program. This activity, with AT&T corporate support, links urban and suburban elementary students across economic, geographical, and racial ethnic lines in a letter exchange. More than 10,000 children have participated. The end of the year get-together unites as many as 3,000 of them in a day of fun and celebration on the William Jewell campus.

Many Jewell alumnae have traveled far from Liberty in their professions. But some who might easily have made their mark in New York or California have stayed "right here in River City," so to speak, and should be classed as "Home Stars."

The nightingale voice of Helen Early could have led her to a professional singing career. Instead, she opted to remain in Liberty as a businesswoman. As an undergraduate she belonged to every vocal group on campus. Thereafter she shared her talents freely, and was a member of the Second Baptist Church choir for seventy-three years; other church work, officership in the Daughters of the American Revolution, and membership on the Alumni Board of Governors are among her activities.

Helen Early receiving her Citation for Achievement

Also reaching out from home was Lutie Chiles. The Jackson County native taught first in rural schools, then in the Kansas City area. With an M.A. from Columbia University and further training at Northwestern University, she became director of elementary education at William Jewell. She originated Elementary Education Day, which annually brought up to 400 elementary teachers to the campus for conferences and lectures. After retirement, she made two trips to Amman, Jordan, as a lay volunteer missionary teacher. For years she managed both the children's and adult libraries of the Second Baptist Church. Asked how many years, she modestly replied, "Oh, so long I can't remember, but Irene La Frenz has done a good part of the work."

Irene La Frenz stayed on home ground, too. Irene Froman, a 1924 graduate, was prominent on the campus when young women were few. Marrying Vern La Frenz, college mathematics professor, she too taught mathematics, at Liberty High School. Her husband said, "She sent me good students." She was also a strong contributor to the activities of her church and college organizations.

Christine Griffey Pugh stayed at home, marrying history professor U.R. Pugh. Her twenty-four years at Liberty High School were not limited to teaching English. Her former students know she

Lutie Chiles' leadership in the elementary education department brought national recognition to William Jewell.

was one of the best. Her good friends call her "Mrs. President," the professional office holder. She has been president of the Fortnightly Study Club, American Association of University Women, Baptist Women and Women's Missionary Union in Liberty, Delta Kappa Gamma, and the Kansas City Browning Society. Work on several state boards has not kept her from serving on the Liberty cemetery and library boards and on college alumni committees.

Lucile Hall Davis emerged as a prominent Liberty businesswoman when few women were found at managerial levels. She owned the Lucile Davis Shop, an exclusive store for women's wear. Active in civic affairs, she worked on city boards and commissions, was a six-term director of the Liberty Chamber of Commerce, president of

Women's basketball team, 1919

Soroptimist International of Liberty, an elder of the Presbyterian Church, William Jewell's Mrs. Alumna, and an Achievement Day honoree.

Vivian Green O'Dell, like Lucile Davis, followed the business route. *The Liberty Shopper News*, under her management, began as a small free-distribution publication and grew to become a major newspaper in Liberty. Her civic involvement includes service to the Liberty Chamber of Commerce, as a leader in helping establish a Liberty sister-city link with Diekirch, Luxembourg, as the Soroptimist Club president, and as a sponsor of a new Northland Soroptimist Club. Immediately upon retirement she enlisted in the Peace Corps for a two-year stint teaching small business management in Lesotho, Africa.

Although not a native of Liberty, Juarenne Moore Hester has stayed here and made notable contributions to the community. After busy undergraduate years, this 1956 graduate earned a graduate degree from the University of Missouri at Kansas City and taught in both the public schools and at William Jewell. Now retired, she has been general chair of the Sesquicentennial Committee. Previously she has served as president of the Liberty Hospital Board, as a member of the Liberty City Council, of the Assistance League, P.E.O., Daughters of the American Revolution, and William Jewell Alumni Association. Perhaps her most challenging and successful activity came as chair of a bond and levy campaign for Liberty public schools.

Becky Speaker Dempsey must have felt quite at home when she entered William Jewell, whose alumni involved her aunt and both of her parents. Becky's triple fields of activity involved extensive church work, service to the college, and drama. A talented character actress, she is a cast member and officer of the Liberty Community Theatre.

Who would think of an art teacher concerning herself with the entire athletic program of a college? That is Nancy Chrisman Jones, a latecomer among women "firsts." As a member of the alumni board of governors, she chaired or co-chaired its athletic commission for six years. This group has rejuvenated alumni interest in the athletic program and developed an alumni athlete "parenting" program. Nancy Jones has contributed hundreds of hours on college phone-athons and in locating lost alumni through computer search.

The spring of 1977 saw the election of Anita McPike Gorman as the second woman president of the alumni association. Less than twenty years later, she was selected as a member of the board of trustees. In those intervening years this Kansas City Northland citizen has led million-dollar campaigns for civic and major service projects. One of her most challenging tasks was, as chair of the Kansas City parks and recreation board, leading the successful campaign for a $50 million upgrade of the Kansas City Zoo. She has been called the "fountain lady," because of her promotion of fountains in the Kansas City area. One particular

Anita Gorman

Audri Adams and Madeline Parrott travel 11,000 miles on a debate trip and are interviewed on NBC.

119

Citations for Achievement

Ms. Ruth Weyand	*Miss Helen Cairnes Early*	*Mrs. Mary Lou Manring Chapman*
Dr. Georgia Bowman	*Mrs. Dorothy Ray White*	*Mrs. Jacqueline Williamson Hollis*
Dr. Mary Elmore Sauer	*Mrs. Rosemary Harrell Jackson*	*Dr. Judith Craig*
Dr. Dorothy A. Truex	*Miss Virginia Dougherty*	*Mrs. Aloah Burke Kincaid*
Mrs. Mary Margaret Jessee Mayfield	*Mrs. Ruth Jessee Strange*	*Dr. Carol Rowland Hogue*
Mrs. Virginia Stuart Ditzen	*Miss Alice Ann Biggerstaff*	*Mrs. Marilyn Chandler Barth*
Mrs. Ora Gaunce Thornberry	*Dr. Carol Ann Reece*	*Mrs. Clara Jones Lowry*
Mrs. Lucille Hall Chiles	*Dr. Joyce Parr Schaie*	*Mrs. Linda J. French*
Mrs. Verlia Short Russell	*Mrs. Francine Coffey Morin*	*Dr. Linda Ehrsam Voigts*
Mrs. Eleanor Burton Harding	*Dr. Mary Jo Smith Evans*	*Miss Joyce E. Shriver*
Mrs. Margaret Davidson Lee	*Mrs. Esther Tateishi Sato*	*Mrs. Marie Duff Stewart*
Dr. Carrie Sprague	*Mrs. Zena Payne Page*	*Mrs. Nancy Warren Fuchs*
Miss Everley Hayes	*Mrs. Dorcas Hauk Fowler*	*Mrs. Patsy Ruth Beltzer*
Mrs. Cyrena Morris Tucker	*Dr. Charlotte Potter Darnell*	*Mrs. Deborah DeLong*
Mrs. Elva Allen Stokes	*Mrs. Anita McPike Gorman*	*Mrs. Augusta E. Hayes*
Miss Wanda L. Ponder	*Mrs. Lucile Hall Davis*	*Mrs. Irene Simon Thomas*
Dr. Constance Burkhardt Nelson	*Dr. Gladys Ward Ritchie*	*Mrs. Diane Betts Adams*
Mrs. Mildred Halferty Bland	*Dr. Lois Schille Eikleberry*	*Ms. Shirley Williams*
Mrs. Ramona Tripp Livingston	*Miss Lutie Chiles, special citation*	*Mrs. Karen McGuigan*
Dr. Rita Dossey Ryan	*Mrs. Jeannie Freeman Maddox*	
Ms. Dorothy Sword	*Dr. Edna Mae Mitchell Steiner*	

fountain area has been named Anita Gorman Park in her honor. She has served as commissioner of the Missouri Department of Conservation and as a board member of the Salvation Army. Her awards and citations number more than a dozen.

Other outstanding women by the dozen could be mentioned here. The list of those who have officially received Citations for Achievement represent the wealth of talent and accomplishments of William Jewell women.

Many influences bear on young people as they emerge to adulthood–some are individuals, some are groups. Often students never realize what forces have had a part in shaping their thinking or providing unseen support or stabilizing their environment.

Aside from actual instructors, staff members mean much to the smooth functioning of college life. Miss Opal Carlin, librarian for thirty-five years, dreamed of a new facility. She saw the demolition of old Carnegie Library and planned the transfer, by 450 students, of 90,000 volumes from the old to the new building. With the opening of Curry Library, women's library segregation was gone forever, but Miss Carlin did not live to know that. She died before the 1965 dedication.

"Campus hostess" describes Mrs. Gladys Davidson. For ten years she and husband Ralph were houseparents at the men's dormitory. After Mr. Davidson's death, "Davey" became housemother successively for Arlington Hall, TNT, and Beta Sigma Omicron. When all the sororities moved into Semple Hall, she was appointed hostess at Yates College Union, and a gracious one she was as she completed thirty-seven years of college affiliation.

Memorable to many students was the cheerful voice of Mrs. Mabel Lozier, helpful switchboard operator for seventeen years, plus another nine as efficient mail clerk. And there was Mrs. Deola Gairrett, registrar for thirty-two years. In the early days of somewhat cumbersome computer service she once noted that she could issue grade reports by hand faster than the early computer could do it.

Her assistant, Mrs. Pat Dillon, remains after thirty-nine years as of 1998, a wealth of knowledge and helpfulness to students in the registrar's office.

The college president's office is not often frequented by students, but when one appears, the greeter was for many years Mrs. Joan Lawrence. For thirty-three years the myriad details of the business of four college presidents have passed through her flexible hands—E.W. Holzapfel, Thomas S. Field, J. Gordon Kingsley, and W. Christian Sizemore. Equally efficient in arranging administrative affairs is Mrs. Nancy Sherrick. Acting as a bulwark for twenty-six years against students demanding to see the academic dean at once is Mrs. Ardi Sharp. Mrs. Ruth Turnage in the student affairs and admissions offices has helped guide several generations of students into the college.

Joan Lawrence, Jewell's "Ambassador" to the President's office, with Dr. Sizemore, 1997

For years, housemothers were the ones who sent coeds back to their rooms for boots and coats in bad weather, who frowned and chided at unseemly noises, and who gave out demerits for rule infractions. Many have come and gone. Four particularly popular housemothers retired the same

Carolyne Geer Hester

year, 1953. They were Mrs. A.G. Byrns, Mrs. Frank Fristoe, Mrs. Grace Stanley, and Miss Mary Mitchell.

Carolyne Geer Hester, along with husband Dr. H.I. Hester, chairman of the religion department, presided over Melrose Hall as houseparents. From Mrs. Hester, a girl learned to be a lady. No girl dared to use loud or boisterous language or run through a corridor. No girl might appear in the dining room in robe or bedroom slippers or hair curlers. One came to meals properly dressed. At each long table, covered with a white cloth, girls took turns as hostesses, passing the bowls of food prepared by mistress-of-the-kitchen, Mrs. Elsie Keller—"Ma." Lights out at midnight (controlled from a central switch). And woe unto the girl whose bed was unmade or whose "secret" coal oil lamp was not hidden in a closet on Monday morning room inspection.

Gone long before the nineties were such rules, and so, too, were motherly housemothers, replaced by young resident directors. However, deans of women abided for many years. The list includes Miss Ruth Lindsey, Miss Ruth McDaniel, Miss

Alma Hunt, Dr. Catherine Bates, Mrs. Dorothy Patterson, and Miss Johnnie Human. Then, no more. Women deans gave way to on overall dean of students.

While they are in school, students may not give much thought to who keeps the campus running. Many women are behind the scenes, largely unknown personally to the men and coeds whose dorms and classrooms they clean, and whose meals they serve, and who plant the flowers that brighten the campus. Without the housekeepers, food service staff, and groundskeepers, the college just would not work.

Ex-officio friends behind the scenes include Betty Shouse '48, who found her career in the Kansas City Public Library. More important to William Jewell have been her many financial contributions, always geared to student improvement.

Involved in the life of the college for many of her more than ninety-nine years was Mrs. Florence Bowles. Of Belgian descent, she became the charming bride of young football coach R.E. Bowles. Active in church work and Faculty Wives, she reared five children. All are William Jewell graduates, as are two daughters-in-law and two grandsons. Impacting strongly on students has been her son, Dr. Richard P. Bowles, for many years the college physician and a member of the board of trustees.

No prizes were awarded to her when in 1963 Mrs. J.L. Downing was the oldest person ever to earn a degree at the college. This she accomplished after a career as a missionary in Brazil.

Three women who never attended William Jewell also had a profound influence. Mrs. Sylvia Kimzey Davis (Colorado Women's College), wife of physics Professor John Davis, was sponsor of TNT sorority, and continued after its affiliation with Alpha Delta Pi. When she died in 1967 she left a son, a daughter, a daughter-in-law, a grandson and his wife, and two granddaughters as Jewell alums.

Working closely with Mrs. Davis on TNT activities, especially the Mothers' and Alumnae Clubs, was Mrs. Miriam Derwacter (Vassar). Dr. Derwacter taught Greek and was the college registrar. The couple had as one of their projects the sponsorship of Phi Epsilon, the local equivalent of Phi Beta Kappa. Mrs. Derwacter also sponsored Sigma Rho.

With the haunting music of her parents' native Russia in her soul, Victoria Unruh Harvey (Fort Hays State College) was a poet whose words sang. Not at all overpowered by the strong personality of her husband, P. Caspar Harvey, English professor, forensics coach, alumni secretary, and public relations director, she had a career in writing all her own. It was as the faithful sponsor of Iota Pi, then Beta Sigma Omicron, then Zeta Tau Alpha, that she left her lasting impression on the many young students who loved her. In addition, the Harvey home was for years the regular meeting place of Sigma Tau Delta literary society.

These three women, along with other college and university graduates in Liberty, carried on a persistent effort to obtain accreditation for the college by the American Association of University Women. Most qualifications had been met, such as adequate library, laboratory, and dormitory facilities. Two items were lacking—a dean of women and a full athletic program for women. These deficiencies were remedied with the appointment of Miss Ruth Lindsey as dean of women in 1936, and employment of Miss Lois Wisler in 1941 as the full-time director of girls' physical education.

As individuals can have large influence on people and events, so can individuals when they are allied in groups.

At the time of World War I, faculty wives found a place for themselves in the Faculty Wives Club under the leadership of the college president's wife, Mrs. John Priest Greene. Ultimately, the group evolved into the Women's Auxiliary, which included both faculty wives and women faculty members.

Women of the secretarial staff organized CORE–College Office Related Employees (as one member laughingly explained, "We didn't want the word 'woman' in the title because some day the administration might hire a male postal clerk or something."). This ongoing group holds monthly luncheon meetings and workshops and has published and marketed two cookbooks.

One day in 1965 several women were enjoying coffee at the home of Mrs. Polly Quick Bowles. "We ought to have some kind of a women graduates organization on the Hill," someone remarked.

That was the beginning of the Woman's Committee, formed to provide service, enhance campus appearance, and foster interest in the college. First president was Mrs. Polly Bowles (always a leader, she was First Lady of the campus her senior year). Other founding members were Louella Reppert, Marilyn Halferty, Dixie Pollard, Irene Thomas, Elise Cooper, Norma Ruth Guilfoil, Carole Johnson, Mary Lou Chapman, and Gertrude Bell. Major projects have included annual women's scholarships and gifts of cultural and artistic acquisitions. Membership includes alumnae, mothers of students, and women friends of the college.

Not a faculty member, not an advisor, not a group member, and never a student, one other woman deserves final mention. Her last name all but forgotten, she was always known as "Aunt Kitty." She presided over Vardeman Dining Hall in the 1890s. At the door she rang the bell for meals and chided those who came late. She brandished her rolling pin at the boys who teased her, ruled over the young men who cut 300 slices of her bread for every meal, and bossed the "preacher boys" who waited tables. Small, wiry, and energetic, queen of her kitchen, Aunt Kitty was William Jewell's "First Lady."

CHAPTER 10

GREEK LIFE

Loyalty, Allegiance, Alma Mater True

by John Truex and Kit Truex Mair

1978 homecoming float

1977 Homecoming Queen, Dee Ann Henry

Memories of almost 128 years (1871-1999) of life as a Greek at William Jewell conjure up many nostalgic moments of various activities in which sororities and fraternities engage during the year. Such a listing is formidable by any standard and would include (but is not limited to):

...summer rush parties ... preschool return to campus and preparation for rush week ... house and meeting room spruce-up ... rush week parties and presentation ... "hot boxes" with rushees ... legacies ... bids for new pledges ... silent period ... Pledge Day ... Greek rallies on the square ... formal pledging ... pledge duties ... pledge parties for the actives ... "Hell Week" (no longer in vogue) ... initiation to active status ... solemn rituals ... intramural athletics ... Homecoming floats and house decorations ... open houses and chili suppers ... informal dances at the house ... pinnings and serenades ... study sessions ... Chapter GPA ... Pledge Fathers ... Big Sisters ... Little Sisters ... Fall formals ... bridge games ... chess games ... Hearts ... phone-a-thon competition ... car washes ... picnics ... trick or treating ... charitable projects at Thanksgiving and Christmas ...

Christmas caroling ... writing a Tatler Revue skit ... practice for Tatler Revue ... winning Tatler Revue (or not) ... Tatler Revue Queens ... Pan-Hellenic ... Interfraternity Council ... Greek Sing Competition ... Quad Games I&II ... CUA Activities Fair ... date dashes ... snowball fights ... picnic dinners ... conviviums ...White Rose Formal ... Founder's Day ... Fiji Weekend ... Old South ... Crown week ... Killarney Ball ... Cow Chip Bingo ... Ronald McDonald ... Special Olympics ... Haydaze ... Black Diamond Ball ... Tahiti Sweetie ... Gay Nineties Party ... Battle of the Bands ... intramural football ... softball ... basketball ... graduation activities ... tearful goodbyes ... alumni dinners ... class reunions ... at five-ten-twenty-five-fifty years-even sixty and seventy years-when sorority sisters and fraternity brothers return and ... remember when!!

And this listing—as incomplete as you alone will recall—includes no time set aside for classes, library,

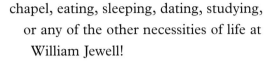

chapel, eating, sleeping, dating, studying, or any of the other necessities of life at William Jewell!

But these activities help bind together a group of individuals into a strong force of good for each other and for themselves. The friendships made last a lifetime as letters, phone calls, and get-togethers forge an even tighter bond of fraternal love with each contact. And now the emergence of the Internet and e-mail opens up an even greater opportunity to stay in touch over the years.

FRATERNITIES

The earliest American society bearing a Greek letter name was Phi Beta Kappa, founded in December 1776 at the College of William and Mary. This had been preceded by a society of somewhat uncertain nature called The Flat Hat, which saw birth in 1750. While that first fraternity (ΦBK) had all the characteristics of a present-day chapter, it became, in about 1820, a school honor society–focusing on scholarship.

Common interests and secret societies have prevailed throughout history, and so it was not unusual that the men of William Jewell would organize groups for both scholarly and social purposes.

The earliest group on the Hill was a literary society called the "Philomathians" founded in 1853, four years after classes were first begun.

With the meager resources of both students and facilities one can be assured that this society was an extracurricular activity. It was spawned by natural competitiveness for both excellence and freedom from classroom discipline, organized by students but carefully guided and supported by the faculty.

In reasonably short order, a competing group, the "Excelsiors," was formed in 1857–no doubt by a number of dissident students who were not invited to become Philomathians. Both of these groups had mottoes, colors, flowers and mascots. Naturally, competition became keen between the two groups—both for members and in the fields of oratory, debate, readings and music. In essence, they were literary societies that helped improve the speaking and presentation skills of many students and aided a great number of ministerial students in the art of pulpiteering. Each group had a meeting room, ornately furnished, on the third floor of Jewell Hall and convened on Friday evenings with reasonable emphasis on social functions so that female companions might be invited.

These two organizations generated the basic thrust of school spirit along with the obvious benefits of public speaking. Both of these groups remained active until the early 1920s but gradually dwindled in members and influence as other campus groups became formalized. Some of these other organizations included Der Deutsche Klub, J Club, Buttinskies, Keen Spitters, Quo Vadis, Square and Compass, state and city clubs and, of course, the senior elite Sons of Rest.

At William Jewell College the fraternity system probably began with the Zeta Phi fraternity, which was brought to the campus from the University of Missouri about 1871. One of the six charter members was J.C. Armstrong '74, who later became college librarian and was known as "Ole Pussyfoot" (probably because he enforced the separate study areas for men from women). Zeta Phi was a secret society of an exclusive nature, with each member given a name of a great man of the past, (e.g., "Francis Bacon," "Carlyle," "Mirabeau," "Disraeli," "Bunyan," etc.). Since this was the only organization of this type on campus, the chapter grew and embraced generally the best students. Meanwhile, the founder of Zeta Phi, Professor Oren Root of the University of Missouri, thought of expanding his fraternity but he soon became more interested in getting his two chapters of Zeta Phi to be taken in as chapters of a national, Phi Gamma Delta. This occurred on April 24, 1886. The national office permitted the Jewell Chapter to become Zeta Phi of Phi Gamma Delta, thus becoming the first fraternity of note to emerge at William Jewell.

About this time there was a "loose" organization of non-fraternity men known as the "Invincible Twenty-Three," whose avowed purpose was antagonistic to the existence of Greek letter fraternities in the college (i.e. Phi Gamma Delta). Nine of these men, after closer study of the college fraternity sys-

tem, came to the conclusion that there was good in fraternities, when properly organized and conducted. They were determined to become a chapter of some college fraternity and bring into practical operation "the ideals which they had conceived." Thus on January 20, 1887, a charter was granted by Kappa Alpha Order to Alpha Delta chapter. While some accounts indicate that "the Phi Gams entertained the KAs at a banquet which was returned in kind," other accounts suggest that "The Fijis instantly accused the initiative of this chapter ... and rivalry between the two orders became intense. For a girl to date a member of Kappa Alpha meant that her name was immediately taken from the Fiji invitation list." Now there were two national fraternities on the Hill.

The third national fraternity, Sigma Nu, had its origin from a local club known as the Phe Yodhs, Hebrew letters for "FJ," which formed the initial letters of the fraternity motto. The Phe Yodhs existed for a year, 1892-93, and then formed a resolve to affiliate with Sigma Nu, which had three chapters in Missouri—at the University of Missouri, Missouri Valley College, and Central College (currently Central Methodist College). So in a private dining room of the historic Coates House in Kansas City on January 6, 1894, Beta Xi chapter of Sigma Nu was chartered at William Jewell College.

In 1897 a fourth fraternity was established on the Hill, that of Kappa Sigma, Alpha Omega chapter. This was the first chapter to be established in

Phi Gamma Delta Chapter house, 1948-

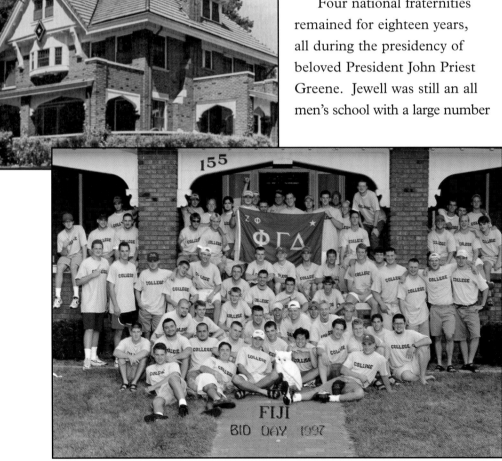

Fiji brothers on bid day, 1997

Missouri. Kappa Sigma left the campus during the Great Depression in 1936 and has not been rechartered. Nonetheless, we include their forty-year history because of the number of men who became affiliated and their importance in the early years of this century.

Four national fraternities remained for eighteen years, all during the presidency of beloved President John Priest Greene. Jewell was still an all men's school with a large number of ministerial students in the student body. In the fall of 1915, the major portion of the inhabitants on New Ely (Third Floor West found themselves bound by a community of interests. Moved by no loftier purpose than a feeling of fellowship and fraternalism, the nine men founded a secret society "Zeta Chi" and for two years existed *sub rosa.* They held regular meetings, pledged and initiated men and, for all intents and purposes, were a fraternity, housed on Third West, decorated in blue and white. By 1917, they had grown to a membership of thirty-one, had developed a constitution and complete ritual and emblems, and on Friday, April 13, 1917, they petitioned the faculty to be recognized as a social fraternity. This request was granted a week later and the official stamp of approval by the college acknowledged the fifth fraternity—albeit a "local" organization. This situation—five fraternities—remained until 1936 when Kappa Sigma lost its charter. Then in 1942, after several possible affiliations with national fraternities had been pursued, Zeta Chi's gained acceptance by Lambda Chi Alpha. Interestingly, Zeta Chi came into existence while the country was engaged in World War I (1917) and Lambda Chi Alpha during World War II (1942). One might have thought this a most unlikely occurrence since many of the men were going into military service.

And so this brief synoptic history outlines the beginnings of fraternities at William Jewell College. Since then these five fine organizations have collectively initiated more than 6,075 men who have an added connection to their loyalty to William Jewell College—a special bond of brotherhood that has grown stronger over the years.

Phi Gamma Delta

Phi Gamma Delta was founded in April, 1848, at Jefferson College in Canonsburg, Pa. The badge, known as the founder's badge, is lozenge shaped, black with a white star above the Greek letters Phi Gamma Delta. The color is royal purple; the flower is the purple clematis. The pledge pin is a white five-pointed star. The flag is rectangular in shape with a white star in the upper right-hand corner of the royal purple background which displays the fraternity's Greek letters. International headquarters are in Lexington, Ky.

Zeta Phi

As stated earlier in the Prologue, the Zeta Phi fraternity was the first social fraternity established at William Jewell College. This (Sigma Chapter) was a branch of the mother chapter at the University of Missouri and was chartered in November, 1871, with six charter members. The chapter was installed at the Arthur House Hotel on the southeast corner of the "square"—considered at that time to be the finest hotel west of the Mississippi. Accounts of the meetings of Zeta Phi include: "Our meetings were held in such vacant rooms as we could find, and usually in darkness ... it was surrounded with a

mystery to its doings ... no one ever got into the secret order who did not have a high standard morally and also a good scholastic record ... no one seemed to know who, when, or where they met, what they did or were trying to do." Perusal of the William Jewell *Student* from 1881 to 1887 shows only minimal reference to any activities of Zeta Phi, although this publication was primarily literary in content.

Phi Gamma Delta- Zeta Phi Chapter

In the mid-1880s both the University of Missouri and William Jewell Chapters of Zeta Phi were considering petitioning larger national fraternities. The University of Missouri (Alpha) chapter joined Beta Theta Pi and Sigma joined Phi Gamma Delta. Both asked to use the name of Zeta Phi as the chapter designation. Both requests were approved, thus perpetuating the old pioneer fraternity.

The Phi Gamma Delta charter at William Jewell was granted on April 24, 1886, followed by a formal installation on May 29 in Excelsior Hall. There were fifteen charter members of this, the fifty-fourth chapter of Phi Gamma Delta.

The first meeting hall rented downtown burned about a month later. Other locations were rented on the square and in town for the next few years until the first home owned by the chapter was purchased in 1913, located at 203 East Mississippi Street. That house served the fraternity well except for two brief periods, one of renovation in 1934-35 following the great Liberty fire of August 10, 1934, and the other following the use by Jewell women during World War II. In 1948 the former Kappa Sigma residence on South Leonard Street was acquired. It housed the fraternity while plans were completed for a move to the new fraternity complex on campus.

Fiji "Rockettes," 1973

Over the years the Phi Gams have established numerous traditions. One of the earliest was the "June Banquet, a gala social occasion which meant fifty cents and a buggy for two or a carriage for four." This gave way to a 'Possum Supper, which was replaced with the Norris Pig Dinner, an evening of fun, fellowship, and reunioning by alumni that continues to this day. Another tradition was associ-

ated with the Tatler Revue, which was founded by Lowell Ditzen '33. For nearly forty years of skits at Tatler Revue the Fijis used a dance line of brothers a la "the Rockettes" and in so doing received more than their share of top awards at Tatler Revue primarily under the alumni supervision of Ray Barr '33.

"Fiji Week" evolved from the older initiation "Hell Week" with its hazing and pranks. This week now became a focus on the history of the fraternity and chapter and the responsibilities of an active member. Special emphasis was placed on local social projects to help the disadvantaged.

Since Phi Gamma Delta was the first fraternity on the Hill, the early days saw an extra number of achievements in various areas of the men's college. At one time the president (Herget), English professor (Fruit), and the venerated librarian (Armstrong) were all Phi Gams. Departments have been endowed and named in honor of Dr. Fruit, Dr. Semple, and Francis Antoine '17. Chairs have been endowed by A. Major Hull '38 and in honor of Wallace A. Hilton '33.

Among the several alumni advisors to Zeta Phi Chapter have been John E. Davis '07, Conn Withers '27, Frank Hester '67, Mike Fligg '61, and Jim Berry '57. A complete history of the chapter was written in 1936 and updated in 1961 by Dr. Wallace A. Hilton '33, honored professor of physics.

The White Science Center as referenced in Chapter 3 was named in honor of John F. White '67, a chairman of the college board of trustees.

As of February 1998 1,556 men have been initiated into Zeta Phi at William Jewell, a proud legion of men who have served their college and fraternity well.

Kappa Alpha Order

Kappa Alpha Order was founded in December 1865 at Washington and Lee University in Lexington, Va. The current badge consists of one gold shield superimposed on another with a Greek cross of gold within the circle with the gold letters KA above on a black field. The colors are crimson and old gold; the flowers are the magnolia blossom and the red rose. The flag consists of three bars of equal width in crimson, white and old gold with a crimson Greek cross on the middle white bar. International headquarters are in Lexington, Va.

The four founders of Kappa Alpha were great admirers of the university president, General Robert E. Lee. They, along with Brother Samuel Zenas Ammen, conceived a ritualistic foundation and pattern of tradition embodied by General Lee, who was then accepted as the "spiritual founder" of the order. Baird's Manual states, "with Ammens' complete revision of the ritual, Kappa Alpha Order was given an identity which set it apart from any other collegiate organization at that time and which still sets it apart."

Lee's image as a "Southern gentleman" has been an enduring symbol to Kappa Alphas, who traditionally observe his birthday on January 19 at Convivium. William Jewell College's former historical museum once boasted as an exhibit a hand-written letter from General Lee to the college's "Excelsior Society." Lee wrote the note in 1868 accepting a proferred membership in that society.

Robert E. Lee, spiritual founder of the Order

Alpha Delta Chapter

As indicated earlier, Alpha Delta of Kappa Alpha was chartered at Jewell on January 20, 1887, to nine men formerly of the anti-Greek "invincible twenty-three." Charter was accepted at the Arthur House, similar to the Phi Gam chartering. Subsequently the chapter began meeting in the office of Dr. William H. Buckley, a dentist who re-entered college and became a charter member of Alpha Delta.

Kappa Alpha Chapter house, 1929-

After several years of meeting in the dental office and rented halls, the chapter rented in 1896 "Hawthorne Institute," at the northwest corner of Water and McCarty Streets, which "pioneered the

131

*Knight Commander
Henry C. Chiles, '07*

Jewell chapter house activity among the fraternities at William Jewell." Over the next twenty years KAs lived in seven different rented houses. In 1916, they became the owners of property at 715 Miller, where they remained until 1921 at which time the South Jewell property was purchased.

The house at 19 South Jewell burned from an overheated furnace in the spring of 1929. Out of the ruins rose the first fraternity house to be constructed at Jewell, admirably designed for fraternity usage and architecturally symbolic of Southern chivalry. This house has served for the last seventy years as the setting for dances, teas, conviviums and other social occasions but mainly as a fraternity residence for chapter members. Originally built to house twenty-six men, the third floor was added to accommodate a total of thirty-six in 1949.

A major social event over many years was the "Old South Ball" in which members obtained Confederate uniforms, horses, and buggies and escorted their appropriately dressed Southern Belles up the front walk for an evening of dancing. On most of these occasions a large Confederate flag was constructed across the entire front porch of the house to add to the atmosphere. The Old South Ball has been significantly altered and is now the "Knights of the Order Ball." Nonetheless, traditional songs about magnolias, Southern sweethearts, and "Dixie" continue to be vocalized from 17 South Jewell to this time.

A special honor was accorded to Henry C. Chiles '07 when he was elected Knight Commander of the entire Kappa Alpha Order and served from 1917-1925. He later served in World War II as a lawyer at the Nuremberg trials in Germany. Other KAs who have served as advisors or major benefactors include Glen Alspaugh '35, Clyde Williams '38, Arthur Reppert '38, Bob Kirkland '38, Fred Benson '53, and in recent years Eric Long '90, Chad Wright '94, and Bob Steinkamp '67. Active at the national order level have been Vance Ecton Rule '49, Bob Steinkamp '67, and Bill Dreyer '60.

A chair in the department of music was endowed by Robert H. McKee '52 and in the department of economics and business administration, by Dr. John W. Boatwright '27. For many years Jewell's athletic director R.E. "Dad" Bowles, father of four KAs, used his shotgun to announce new pledges. To this day, many KAs have the cartridge of their pledgeship.

As of February, 1998, 1,559 men have been initiated into the Alpha Delta Chapter of Kappa Alpha at William Jewell, all proud knights of Southern chivalry who have loyally served their order and their alma mater.

New Sigma Nu Chapter house, 1998

Sigma Nu brothers display portrait of Terry Straeter

Sigma Nu Chapter house, 1904-1968

Sigma Nu

Sigma Nu was founded on January 1, 1869, at the Virginia Military Institute in Lexington, Va., which is now the home of its international headquarters. Organization proceeded from VMI's Legion of Honor dedicated to the eradication of hazing and other immature practices. Honor has been the cardinal principle over the years, along with truth and love. The badge is a five-armed cross resembling the French medal, the *legion d'honour*; the serpent, crossed swords, and gold letters display the governing code. The colors are black, white, and gold and the flower is the white rose. The flag consists of three horizontal bars of black, white, and gold with a coiled golden serpent in the center.

Beta Xi Chapter

With two national fraternities at the college in 1892 (Phi Gams and KA), a group of Jewell men formed a local society known as the Phe Yodhs, Hebrew letters for "FJ," which formed the initial letters of the group's motto (Friends of Jewell, maybe?). After a year as a local club, Joseph E. Culver led a resolve to have the group affiliate with Sigma Nu, which then had nearby chapters at the University of Missouri, Missouri Valley College, and Central Methodist College. Thus on January 6, 1894, the Beta Xi chapter, the forty-third in Sigma Nu, received its charter in installation ceremonies at the historic Coates House in Kansas City. Beta Xi's first meetings, like those of the other fraternities, were held in rented quarters downtown on the square, in a hall over a store on

133

East Kansas Street. After five years, the chapter moved to the Major Alvan Lightburne house on North Water Street, a Georgian ante-bellum residence reputed at one time to be the oldest fraternity house west of the Mississippi. Legend over the years also had suggested a tunnel from the sub-basement of the house to the Missouri River, which was part of the slave "underground railroad" operating during the Civil War period. Older members indicate this part of the house was also used for part of the initiation ceremonies. For more than fifty years, this home served the fraternity in the various functions of the chapter until it finally became unsafe for student housing.

A major contribution to the overall fraternity picture at William Jewell came as a result of a smallpox epidemic that broke out in 1900. One of the Sigma Nu brothers was stricken and the health authorities of Liberty sought to place a quarantine on the house. The 1931 *Tatler* states: "A few hours later the entire chapter had been installed several miles from town in a tent. In a tent the chapter lived for several weeks, at first waiting for others to be stricken, finally relaxing from the tension to enjoy the freedom from classwork provided by this change of habitat. Foods of many kinds, perhaps even fine drink, did Kappa Alpha, Phi Gamma Delta, and Kappa Sigma send to the stranded brethren of Beta Xi. Greatly was this food appreciated. In demonstration a banquet did the brothers of Beta Xi give to the three fraternities when quarantine was lifted, and forth from this mellowness and friendliness emerged the Pan-Hellenic Council" (later changed to the Inter-fraternity Council which exists to the present time).

In 1969 the former Norton-Crawford house on Moss Avenue on the west side of Liberty, near the site of the Old Liberty Ladies College, was purchased by the Sigma Nus. This large home served as the chapter house until 1996 when it was deemed necessary to move to other quarters. It had become evident by 1989 that a move would soon be necessary and efforts began under the leadership of Terry Straeter '64 to purchase an alternate site close to the college. The result of his efforts and beneficence led to the decision to build a fraternity complex for all fraternities on land owned by the college. Because the Sigma Nus had begun their plans early on, the Beta Xi Chapter House was constructed in 1997 and occupied in January 1998. It is a magnificent edifice, located north of the college on property given to William Jewell by Will P. Browning '06, a Sigma Nu and a long-time trustee and major benefactor of the college. His name is honored on Browning Hall and Browning Theater, and the part of the campus donated by him includes the baseball field, the soccer field, and golf course.

Lambda Chi Alpha Chapter house, 1958-1996

A high point for Beta Xi came in 1936 and 1937 when in consecutive years it received the Gallagher Cup for achieving the highest scholarship of all Sigma Nu Chapters. This was followed in 1939 by the selection of Maurice Winger and John Breckenridge as the two United States intercollegiate debaters to debate in England at Oxford and Cambridge. This was the crowning forensics achievement of P. Caspar Harvey '10, venerable English professor, debate coach, and public relations director who was a long-time Sigma Nu advocate and who was later made an honorary initiate.

Another trustee and benefactor was Hubert Eaton '02, who founded Forest Lawn Cemetery in Los Angeles. Eaton Hall is named for his father who was a professor at William Jewell College for nearly thirty years.

Loyal alumni advisors over the years have included Frank Hamilton 1898, Sam Church '26, Frank Millen '33, and in recent years, Larry Kanning '66.

From its founding in 1894 to February 1998, 1,210 men have been initiated into Beta Xi Chapter. They are a loyal and honorable group of alumni of the fraternity and the college.

Lambda Chi Alpha

Lambda Chi Alpha was founded at Boston University on November 2, 1909. The badge of the fraternity is a pearl-set crescent with horns turned toward the left and enclosing a monogram of the Greek letters ΛΧΑ. The center of the crescent bears the Greek letters ΔΠ in gold on black enamel. The colors are purple, green, and gold. The flower is the white rose. The flag consists of a purple ground displaying, between three five-pointed stars in chevron, a cross bearing a shield and the Greek letters ΛΧΑ behind which is a waxing crescent moon.

Zeta Chi

The original Zeta Chi, the forerunner local fraternity to Lambda Chi Alpha, is strictly William Jewell in nature. In the fall of 1915 nine men housed on Third Floor West of New Ely Hall founded a secret society which existed *sub rosa* as a "Club" for nearly two years. Zeta Chi held regular meetings, pledged men, initiated them in their blue and white colors, and imitated the four national fraternities then on campus of this all-men's college.

On Friday April 13, 1917, the Club petitioned

the faculty for permission to exist openly as a fraternity on the Hill. This was granted on April 20, even in the midst of World War I and the loss of many men to the military services.

At the beginning of that school year, the chapter moved for three years to a rented home which had previously been rented by the KAs and Kappa Sigs. The chapter then moved to 225 North Lightburne Street, a property which the chapter purchased and remained in for the duration of Zeta Chi.

From the outset, this group of men were recognized for their scholarship even though they participated in a full social program. The chapter regularly led all other fraternities in grades and in the number of student assistants. An early member, O.K. "Dimp" Evans '20 was the first athlete in William Jewell's history to receive letters in five major sports. Later, his widow endowed a chair in the education department.

During the twenty-five years of its existence as a "local" fraternity, Zeta Chi initiated about 300 men who were loyal to the ideals of both the fraternity and William Jewell. One of the key alumni was Kyle Bales '18, who was the first pledge of Zeta Chi and later became alumni secretary and directed the nationalization of Zeta Chi into Lambda Chi Alpha. Another prominent alumnus was Garnett M. Peters II '29, who donated the Peters Theater in Brown Hall. John and William Linville, two Zeta Chi alumni noted for their scholarship and excellent careers in science, were the only twins honored with William Jewell's Citation for Achievement.

Lambda Chi Alpha (Epsilon Nu Chapter)

In the fall of 1941, after a thorough investigation of other options, the members of Zeta Chi petitioned the Grand High Zeta of Lambda Chi Alpha for membership, which was consummated in impressive ceremonies on May 22-23, 1942. Some eighty-five undergrads and alumni were initiated, one of the largest charter groups of Lambda Chi Alpha.

Due to World War II, the next four years were bleak in many respects; at one point there were only three active members. The Navy came to the campus and took over the dormitories, forcing the women to move into other fraternity houses, and the Zeta Chi house became "home" for the remaining KAs and Fijis. Finally, the limitations of rationing and other wartime restrictions greatly hampered the normal social activities.

After the war, good times returned and membership increased to the extent that new dining and sleeping facilities were added. Nonetheless, a bigger house was needed, and in 1958 the chapter moved to a house at 449 East Kansas, closer to the campus. This house, even though cramped at the time (as were all others), served the chapter well until a fire in 1996 destroyed it. Following the fire, the fraternity made plans to construct a new house at the fraternity complex on college ground northwest of the baseball field.

Campus and alumni honors have been numerous over the years with primary recognition of scholarship, an obvious legacy from Zeta Chi. At one point in the late '60s, Epsilon Nu had captured the inter-fraternity scholarship cup for eighteen out of twenty-one years. Between 1977 and 1986, the chapter achieved four Grand High Alpha awards, the highest honor in Lambda Chi Alpha. Being eligible for the award only once every three years, the chapter is one of the few Lambda Chi chapters to win the award four consecutive times.

Mentioned earlier in Zeta Chi was the influence of Kyle Bales who led the chapter into Lambda Chi Alpha. One of the prominent alumni is Dr. Richard Harriman '53, an English professor and co-founder of the William Jewell Fine Arts Program. He has served as alumni advisor for over thirty years and was recognized by the International Fraternity in 1984 with its highest service award, the Order of Merit.

As of February 1998, 1,071 men have been initiated into Epsilon Nu, which includes some former Zeta Chi members. The chapter has a proud heritage of brotherhood that has flourished into a strong and distinguished group of William Jewell alumni.

Kappa Sigma

Kappa Sigma was established as an extension of, and was named for, a secret organization at the University of Bologna in Italy, which was organized in A.D. 1400 for protection against the wicked governor of the city. On December 10, 1869, three men at the University of Virginia who had studied at Bologna established Kappa Sigma in the United States with a strong tradition of Jeffersonian democracy.

Marlin (Jim) Davis '29, Kappa Sig, "Jock" Ewing of the "Dallas" TV series in the 1970s and '80s. He is arguably Jewell's most recognized alumnus.

The badge is a crescent surmounted by a five-point star within which are the letters KΣ the general surface being convex in form. On the crescent, a skull and bones are above the star, crossed swords are on one side, and crossed keys are on the other side. The pledge button is a triangle bearing the caduceus surmounted by a circle with the letters KΣ enclosed.

The colors are scarlet, white, and green. The flower is the lily of the valley. The coat of arms includes a shield with a five-starred bend sinister and a crescent moon, a circle-surmounted caduceus over the shield and the letters ΑΕΚΔΒ on a ribbon under the shield. The flag consists of three equal width vertical bars of scarlet, white, and green with the coat of arms on the middle bar.

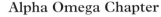

Alpha Omega Chapter

The fourth national fraternity established on Jewell's campus was the Alpha Omega chapter of Kappa Sigma in 1897, the sixty-first chapter of the fraternity. There were seven charter members.

Like the other fraternities before them, the Kappa Sigs' first home was on the courthouse square, as were their next two. Between 1897 and 1931, Alpha Omega moved ten times, a William Jewell record. The final move was to 155 South Leonard Street, later to become "home" to the Phi Gams.

As indicated earlier, this account is more abbreviated than the others, because the chapter ceased operations in 1936. However, up to that time 379 men had been initiated into Alpha Omega including many young men of prominent Liberty families.

Outstanding alumni were Clarence Cannon '04, later a U.S. Congressman and confidant of President Truman. Manley O. Hudson '06, who edited the first *Tatler* in 1905, went on to become dean of the Harvard Law School, legal secretary of the League of Nations, and the only American judge on the World Court at Geneva.

Mr. Hudson also left a legacy to William Jewell that remains legendary to this day. In 1906, as class president, he planted at Class Day Exercises an ivy vine on the north side of Jewell Hall. The vine has graced that wall for as long as any readers of this chapter can remember.

The department of chemistry was named in honor of another Kappa Sig, James Andrew Yates '27.

Another member of the Kappa Sigs was Marlin (Jim) Davis '29 an outstanding athlete at Jewell who went on to a career in Hollywood and then became "Jock" Ewing of the "Dallas" TV series in the 1970s and '80s. He is arguably Jewell's most recognized alumnus.

Though this chapter ceased operations in 1936, the 379 men who had worn the badge were proud patriots of their country, college, and fraternity. Several members are still living who remember their fraternity days at William Jewell with great pride.

SORORITIES

When one considers that William Jewell was a "men only" campus for the first seventy years of its 150-year existence, it is refreshing to see how much "added value" women brought to the campus and how sororities have enhanced the overall quality of life on the Hill in the last eighty years. One can only feel sympathetic for those fellows who constantly yearned (and prayed) for the college to become coeducational, although there were many men, both students and alumni, who opposed coeducation. In fact, essays in the *Student* as early as 1880 were openly advocating the advantages of a coeducational existence, and the *Tatler* of 1909 includes pictures of two sororities, Beta Sigma Omicron and Eta Epsilon Gamma, without any notation or explanation. (They were from the Liberty Ladies College.)

It is not surprising that once the college opened its doors to admit women (in 1917, during the peak of World War I) those who enrolled felt a need to organize a group dedicated to common goals and ideals and, perhaps, begin to "change some of the old traditions of the college."

So it was that Iota Pi was formed in 1919 when there were fewer than fifty coeds on the Hill. Even so, it took until 1920 for the group to receive faculty approval, and for two years it was the only sorority on the campus. Iota Pi remained a local until September 1931, when it became affiliated with Beta Sigma Omicron, a national sorority that had its origin in the state of Missouri in 1888. In fact, a chapter of Beta Sigma Omicron was active for six years at Liberty Ladies College, a women's college that existed on the hill at the then west edge of Liberty. That building burned in 1913 and, despite several unsuccessful attempts to reopen and rebuild, the college ceased to operate. No doubt this was a prime impetus for the official admission of women to William Jewell, since the majority of students at Liberty Ladies College were residents of Liberty or nearby towns. In any event, numerous Beta Sig alumni in town were helpful in the transition of Iota Pi into Beta Sigma Omicron, Alpha Psi Chapter.

Beta Sigma Omicron, a national sorority, had its beginnings in junior colleges, even some high schools, with primary emphasis on "the genteel arts of being a lady: music, painting, elocution, dress-making, rather than academic subjects." The evolution from junior colleges to senior colleges, the national Depression of the '20s and '30s, World War II, and active competition from other larger groups, found Beta Sigma Omicron in 1963 with only twelve active chapters.

In order to preserve the existence of the sorority, Beta Sigma Omicron decided that the best course of action would be to merge with sisters of Zeta Tau Alpha, an organization founded in 1898 at Longwood College in Virginia. That merger was completed in August, 1964, and Zeta Tau Alpha has been on the William Jewell campus since that time.

With the entrance of women into Jewell, enrollment increased from that source as well as from the return of soldiers from World War I. The "roaring '20s" brought change to the campus: a new president, new buildings, and a new sorority.

TNT was organized as a club in 1922 by seven Jewell women who were also residents of Liberty. This local influence persisted strongly throughout the early decade of TNT in which two-thirds of the members were graduates of Liberty High School.

The "club TNT" existed for three years before it was officially acknowledged as a sorority; thus, in the 1920s there were two local sororities on campus. TNT thrived, along with the Iota Pi/Beta Sigs, but decided that it would be better to be affiliated with

139

The ADPis' and Phi Gams' skit—sporting a huge newspaper with moveable headlines—captured Tatler Revue's second place trophy in 1964.

a national sorority. The chapter had been "courted" by several organizations over the years and finally agreed in 1949 to become Gamma Nu chapter of Alpha Delta Pi.

The close of World War II, the activation of the G.I. Bill, and the general acceptance of college education as a standard saw most institutions of learning increase dramatically in the late 1940s. With the enrollment of male veterans in unprecedented numbers, it was only natural that more women would come to college. This was also true at Jewell. It was also the right time for sororities to expand as nationals sought new campuses to expand their chapters.

Thus, in 1946 Alpha Gamma Delta was established with ten charter members, the first totally new Greek organization in thirty years.

As enrollment at William Jewell steadily increased and the ratio of women to men also grew, there was

a perceived need for another sorority on campus.

Delta Zeta came to campus in 1961 and was the final sorority to be established at William Jewell. This brought the number of sororities to four, matching the number of active fraternities. This equation facilitated campus social activities such as Homecoming, Campus Sing, Tatler Revue skits, and other events.

Meeting rooms for sororities have been provided by the college since the late 1920s when Melrose dormitory was completed and all women from out of town were required to live in the dorm.

An early exception was the "quasi-house" of the TNTs in 1929. Then from 1948 to 1957 with the large increase in students, and a lack of women's dormitory space, the college acquired three houses adjacent to the campus, which were designated as sorority houses for the ADPis, Beta Sigs, and Alpha Gams.

Following completion of Semple Hall in 1957, each sorority was provided a wing and a meeting room for which furnishings are provided by each sorority.

Since 1919, the number of women initiated into sororities totals approximately 4,779. The common bonds of sisterhood serve to enhance their loyalty and allegiance to their alma mater.

Zeta Tau Alpha

Zeta Tau Alpha (Fraternity) was founded on October 15, 1898, at Longwood College, Farmville,

Va., and chartered by the Virginia Legislature on March 5, 1902.

The badge is a shield with a smaller black shield raised upon it. In the center is a five-pointed crown, flanked by the initials ZTA. The colors are turquoise blue and steel gray. The flower is the white violet. The "open" motto is "Seek the noblest."

Zeta Tau Alpha at William Jewell is descended from two previous organizations.

Iota Pi (1919-1931)

Iota Pi was formed in 1919 at a time when there were less than fifty coeds on the Hill. While the maintenance of a high standard of scholarship was primary, the second ideal was to provide social and campus activities for its members, which it did in singular fashion. The initial crest of Iota Pi formed a shield divided into four sections. In one section was a heart, in another a rose; a third contained an open vessel in which burned a flame, while the fourth contained a ship's anchor.

By 1927, the crest had been revised to a triangle on which was displayed a set of balanced scales under which was a closed lamp with flame; the open rose symbol was above the triangle with a scrolled Iota Pi at the bottom. By that time there were twenty-three members and pledges and eighteen alumnae in the city of Liberty.

The pin was the letter Π in gold over which the I in black enamel was superimposed and beset with

five pearls. The flower was the red rose and the colors, red and white. The sponsor was Mrs. P. Caspar Harvey, in whose home most of the meetings were held.

Beta Sigma Omicron (1931-1964)

In 1931 the Beta Sigma Omicron chapter president was Miss Georgia Bessie Bowman, who was instrumental in leading Iota Pi into becoming a member of a national organization. As mentioned earlier, Beta Sigma Omicron had been founded at the University of Missouri in 1888 and had established the Omicron Chapter at Liberty Ladies College in 1908. Its Liberty existence on an active basis ended when the Ladies College burned in 1913, but there were many alumnae in Liberty and nearby surroundings who were both interested in and able to help take Iota Pi into Beta Sigma Omicron, the twenty-third chapter active at that time. Installation took place in a two-day ceremony including a gala dinner at the Party Place. Miss Bowman became the Beta Sigs' first president of the Alpha Psi Chapter and has remained as a loyal advisor and counselor for almost seventy years. The Georgia B. Bowman chair in communication was established in 1993 in honor of her distinguished teaching career at the college.

As the only national sorority on campus until 1949, when the TNTs became ADPis,

the Beta Sigs captured their share of pledges, campus honors, queens, and other recognition for the next thirty-three years. Besides Miss Bowman '34, Anita Gorman '53 and Norma Guilfoil '52 were especially active in advising and counseling the chapter. Miss Bowman was active at the national level, serving as editor of the *Urn* from 1936 to 1942 and as national president from 1942 to 1946. Norma Guilfoil was first vice president of the Grand Council in 1963-64 when the Beta Sigma Omicron sorority united with Zeta Tau Alpha fraternity on August 6, 1964. From 1931 until then, the Alpha Psi Chapter had initiated 688 women into its membership.

Alpha Delta Pi house

Zeta Tau Alpha - Delta Chi Chapter

The toll of the Great Depression and World War II, plus the active competition of sororities with more chapters, found Beta Sigma Omicron in 1963 with only twelve active chapters. After difficult and emotional review of their situation, the Grand Council recommended a merger with Zeta Tau Alpha. Dr. Bowman was chair of the special committee.

So Delta Chi became the 119th chapter of Zeta Tau Alpha and has continued during the last thirty-five years to be a campus leader in the many activities of Greek women on the campus.

Since 1964, 859 women have been initiated into Delta Chi Chapter of Zeta Tau Alpha, including women from Beta Sigma Omicron and Iota Pi.

Alpha Delta Pi

The first secret sisterhood for college women was Alpha Delta Pi, founded in 1851 at Wesleyan Female College in Macon, Ga., the oldest women's college in the world. Originally chartered as the Adelphean Society, the name was changed to Alpha Delta Phi Omega in 1905 in the Superior Court of Georgia, Bibb County. This presented a problem for several years because a men's fraternity had the same name. The women again petitioned the court. On April 11, 1914, the sorority became Alpha Delta Pi.

The Adelphean founders chose as their open motto, "We live for each other," and their avowed purpose was that of bettering themselves "morally, mentally and socially." Many of the traditions and much of the ritual of Alpha Delta Pi are the same today as in 1851. Alpha Delta Pi encourages service projects on both levels, collegiate and alumnae. For many years the sorority heavily supported the National Crippled Children's Association. During the past eighteen years Alpha Delta Pi has aided and supported the Ronald McDonald Houses as its national philanthropy and service project.

The badge is a diamond of black enamel over gold displaying at the top portion clasped hands. At the east-west points is a star and beneath are the letters ΑΔΠ. The pledge pin is gold bearing the Greek letters ΒΥΑ, surmounted by a demi-lion, that is, the head and shoulder portion of the lion with the front paws raised. The colors are azure blue and white, and the flower is the single purple woodland violet. Permanent headquarters for Alpha Delta Pi are in Atlanta, Ga., but from 1948 to 1954 the offices were in Kansas City, Mo. Mrs. Joy Scarborough Crouch of Liberty, Mo., served as Omicron Province President from 1963-1971.

TNT (1922-1949)

The forerunner of Alpha Delta Pi at Jewell was a local sorority organized in 1922 by seven women who were also residents of Liberty. TNT possessed an early tradition that was much a part of Liberty High School, from which it drew a majority of its earliest members.

For the first three years, TNT existed as a

ADPi Homecoming, 1964

"club" before it was officially recognized as a sorority by administration officials. The *Tatler* of 1931 carries the following historical comment: "There is, quite likely no more than a vague psychological relation between the meaning of TNT's name, and the meaning, composition, and functions of trinitrotoluene, but it is also conceivable that without the widespread use of trinitrotoluene during the World War I, the sorority of TNT would not now be so designated. Traditionally guarding the secret of its name, there was a time when speculation as to its meaning was widespread."

The sorority (club) designated the violet as her flower (psychic perhaps since that is also the flower of Alpha Delta Pi) and her colors were lavender and purple. The first sign of a pin or crest appeared in the 1924 *Tatler* as a shield upheld by olive branches topped by the head of an armored

143

Alpha Gamma Delta house

knight. This was changed in 1926-27 to a beveled triangle of black enamel with one letter inscribed in each angle and the Greek word A'per N in the middle. The crest includes four stars, a scroll topped by a crown and upheld by the Roman numerals of the founding year.

From the initial seven members, TNT steadily grew in number and activities as well as competitively as a local sorority on the Hill. Teas, breakfasts, receptions, parties, and dances became routine despite the Depression years and the varying challenges of World War II.

The TNTs possessed a "quasi-chapter house" on Miller Street in 1929-30. Chapter meetings and a few social events were held there. But in the fall of 1930, the college required that all non-Liberty coeds reside in Melrose Hall and chapter rooms were provided for the sororities. These rooms were furnished at the sororities' expense, as they are today.

TNT women were active in all aspects of student life, serving as officers of clubs and honor groups as well as editors and business managers of student publications. Naturally, they had their share of Tatler, Homecoming, Carnival queens and

war bond sales, and participated fully in parades and Tatler Revue. Traditionally, the TNTs rode on the Liberty fire truck in the Homecoming parade.

An active alumnae chapter assisted the women during Rush Week and with the traditional Mother's Day Teas and other special occasions. Sponsors of TNT included Mrs. Sylvia Davis, Mrs. Miriam Derwacter, Mrs. Myrl Remley as well as loyal, local alumnae Lucille Davis and Helen Early.

With most men in military service during World War II the social life of the campus was heavily dependent on sorority activities. Following the war, as the veterans returned, more women students came to the college and national sororities began to expand to other campuses. TNT had been courted by several national sororities and in 1949 became affiliated with Alpha Delta Pi.

Up to that time TNT had initiated 414 members into the William Jewell Chapter.

Alpha Delta Pi - Gamma Nu Chapter (1949-present)

In its twenty-sixth year on the Jewell campus, TNT became the seventy-fourth chapter of Alpha Delta Pi in installation ceremonies on April 23, 1949, shortly before the centennial of William Jewell and only two years prior to the centennial of Alpha Delta Pi. Gamma Nu has had the distinction of seeing one initiate serve as Grand President of Alpha Delta Pi. She is Margaret MacDonald Bundy, who graduated from William Jewell in 1964.

Since 1949, 1,037 women have been initiated into Gamma Nu Chapter at William Jewell.

Alpha Gamma Delta

Alpha Gamma Delta was founded as a sorority on May 30, 1904, at Syracuse University by eleven young women who had the vision to see the need for an organization that could make a difference.

The badge is a monogram design of the three Greek letters, ΑΓΔ, with the delta plain, the gamma engraved, and the alpha superimposed upon the two and set with pearls or diamonds or unjeweled. The pledge pin is on a shield, parti per pale or and vert per fess executed in red, buff, and green enamel. The colors are red, buff, and green; the flowers, red and buff roses. International headquarters are in Indianapolis, Ind.

Epsilon Epsilon Chapter

The third sorority to be chartered at William Jewell was Alpha Gamma Delta on October 26, 1946, the fifty-third chapter of the sorority. This occurred following World War II as both male veterans and females entered colleges in record numbers. There were obvious limitations as to the practical size of the two existing sororities and so the opportunity existed for another organization.

Miss Pat Davis, one of the outstanding debaters of that time, began investigating other sororities that might be interested in coming to the Jewell campus.

Alpha Gamma Delta sisters

Contact with Alpha Gamma Delta was soon established and the chapter at the University of Missouri was visited by Pat and several others who had become interested. The national requirement that there be ten members was quickly satisfied and approval was granted by both the national sorority and the college. Of the ten charter members of 1946, eight were alive and well in early 1998.

Recognition of the first addition to the Greeks in almost twenty-five years was celebrated by a dance at the Sigma Nu house given by the Panhellenic and Inter-fraternity Councils. The first installation of new pledges was held in January, 1947, at a Feast of Roses banquet. Six new initiates and two honorary members were initiated and the

October 1946 initiation for sisters of Alpha Gamma Delta

Alpha Gams were well underway to becoming a complete addition to the history and culture of William Jewell College.

At the national level Alpha Gams have been very active in supporting the Easter Seal Society and the Association for Children with Learning Disabilities, both American and Canadian. The Founders Memorial Foundation gives scholarship grants at the graduate and undergraduate level.

Since 1946, Epsilon Epsilon Chapter has initiated 957 members, all true to the ideals of Alpha Gamma Delta and William Jewell College. Epsilon Epsilon Chapter has continued to be a strong and active chapter, owing to the hard work and dedication of its undergraduate members as well as the active involvement of its alumnae.

Delta Zeta

Delta Zeta was founded at Miami University, Oxford, Oh., on October 24, 1902. The badge is a Roman lamp resting upon an Ionic column, hanging upon each side are three wings of Mercury. The official jeweling is a diamond in the flame, with four pearls at the base of the lamp. The lamp bears the sorority's Greek letters, ΔZ, in black enamel. The diamond-shaped pledge pin of black enamel bears the Roman lamp in gold. International headquarters are in Columbus, Oh.

The colors of Delta Zeta are old rose and green; the flower is the Killarney rose. A contemporary mascot for the sorority is the turtle.

Zeta Rho Chapter

Delta Zeta was organized at William Jewell College in 1961 by a local sorority that decided to become national. The sorority, the latest Greek organization to come to campus, balanced in number the national sororities with the four fraternities, which simplified cooperation with counterpart organizations.

The William Jewell chapter is named Zeta Rho. In keeping with the areas of emphasis embraced by Delta Zeta nationally, the William Jewell chapter promotes several philanthropic events each year. The speech and hearing impaired community is the international philanthropy of Delta Zeta. Local charities are promoted each year through the chapter as well as events to support Gallaudet University.

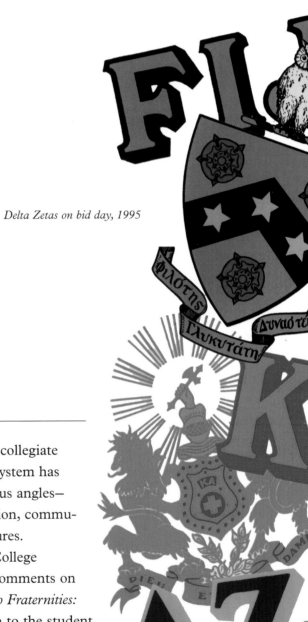

Delta Zetas on bid day, 1995

The Zeta Rho women's social activities include the fall Shindig and a spring formal, known as the Killarney Ball.

Zeta Rho chapter has been successful in its province, and has received the Outstanding Chapter Award given to the most successful chapter in the state. In 1996, the chapter received the highest award given Delta Zeta nationally, the Council Award. This award is presented to chapters who repeatedly achieve a level of excellence (both on the state and national level) in academic achievement, philanthropic support, standards development, and socially.

In recent years, several Delta Zeta women have been selected as Kansas City Chiefs cheerleaders.

Since 1961, 731 women have been initiated into the Zeta Rho Chapter of Delta Zeta.

EPILOGUE

From the earliest days of collegiate organizations, the fraternity system has been under attack from various angles—students, faculty, administration, communities, and even state legislatures.

A 1923 publication on "College Fraternities" includes some comments on the *Basics of Past Opposition to Fraternities:* "The real cause of opposition to the student secret societies of this time was the atmosphere of distrust and narrow sectarianism in which the faculty minds had been reared. When they had been students, there had been no such thing as individual liberty or

1987 Pledge Class of Delta Zeta

others are vigorous in their defense. Generally speaking, however, this has not been a serious issue at William Jewell."

In the William Jewell *Bulletin* of October 15, 1929, is found this statement: "The chapters of these fraternities and sororities have meant much to William Jewell and mean a great deal at the present time. They are controlled and governed under specific and rigorous faculty regulations, and all the popularly considered excesses of fraternity and sorority life have been eliminated from our campus— William Jewell is proud of its fraternities and sororities, and they in turn are proud of William Jewell. These work together to establish an *esprit de corps* which produces great benefits to the entire enrollment of the student body."

Dr. Hester continues: "The record will show that through the years the men and women belonging to the Greek letter organizations have given a good account of themselves. They have demonstrated a loyalty to the College while students and many of them have shown continued interest in the college after graduation. In this number are many men and women who have attained prominence and who give time, thought, and financial support to their alma mater."

"Fast forward" to 1980 in a report to the college board of trustees prepared by the student affairs staff. This document lists nine educational values and needs of students met by the fraternities and sixteen specific services to the college and commu-

individual responsibility; and they still believed that the new generation should conform to the restricted conditions as they themselves had done a generation before."

Criticism of the fraternities (and sororities) was categorized and discussed under these headings:

Snobbishness, Irreligious, Clannishness,
College politics, Extravagance,
Preference to athletes, Indolence, Immorality,
Scholarship, Discipline

Organizations at Jewell have not been immune to criticism, as would be particularly natural for a school allied with Baptists. In his book, *Jewell Is Her Name*, published in 1969, H.I. Hester writes: "The question of fraternities and sororities in college life has always been one on which there are differences of opinion. Some are opposed to these;

nity. Excerpts from this report include the following statements: "The fraternity system at William Jewell College offers a viable and absolutely necessary option for the student body. It is easy, and in many cases, very important to identify with the idealism of the brotherhood and group acceptance for the individual. Any college social structure must maintain at least the option to allow students to choose some type of group identity. The fraternity system as a general rule helps in retaining students. The system is an organized fashion for students to serve the community and the college."

Despite these many advantages, the report indicated that the fraternities "create problems for the college," for example, lower housing standards, violation of college policies, and abrasive standards of conduct to the community.

However, with the establishment of a fraternity complex on college property in 1998, and with the Sigma Nus occupying the first house, it is believed that these negatives will be eliminated or minimized. The substandard living conditions are being replaced by magnificent $2 million-plus houses, half funded by the college. This contribution, along with the negotiated leases, indicates a willingness on the part of both groups to upgrade the system and enhance the overall image of the fraternities at William Jewell.

Returning to the affirming part of the 1980 report: "The greatest service which fraternities provide is directed to the individual member to mature socially and intellectually. It is here that the student learns to assume responsibilities for his own actions while showing concern for others. The relationships in a fraternity house enrich this learning process far beyond the capacity of a dormitory residence. The incredible capacity of fraternities is in the area of personal development. Many leaders, once reticent and relatively inactive, arise to plan large events, manage money, and deal effectively with peers. Notably less dramatic, yet possibly most important, is the fact that one finds through the fraternity sincerely good friends—friendships that may last a lifetime. The same man in all probability would be poorer in this area without his fraternity."

And these same comments apply equally to the sorority system at William Jewell, save for the substandard housing, since sorority housing has been provided in college dormitories for the past seventy years.

May the Greek system continue to positively contribute to students for the next 150 years of William Jewell College.

Loyalty, allegiance, alma mater true.

CHAPTER 11

JEWELL AND COMMUNITY

Working, Trusting, Onward

by Daniel Lambert

*O*n the eve of its sesquicentennial William Jewell stands among the finest of America's liberal arts colleges. Its programs are highly regarded by its peers, and its graduates have impacted the world well beyond what their modest numbers might suggest. It is a good college.

William Jewell has also distinguished itself as a contributing member of the communities it serves and as an effective corporate partner in civic and cultural affairs. This critical dimension of institutional life evolved gradually. In its early years, mostly set apart from its host community, the college identified almost exclusively with its Baptist constituency and seemed driven very little by town-gown considerations. However, as the college matured and its people became active in the local community, the college embraced this as its most important constituency. Thus, while loyal to its religious heritage, William Jewell assumed an increasingly greater role in community affairs.

After World War II, the college slowly emerged as an important force in the rapidly expanding metropolitan area. The isolation the college so much enjoyed early on has today given way to the reality of its obligation to surrounding communities. As a result, greater Kansas City now looks to William Jewell to affirm those values that are essential to humanity: compassion, dignity, justice, and hope. It turns to the college, too, for a perspective on its place in history, for its sense of beauty and vision and, if cities can be said to have one, for its very soul.

STEEPLE AND TOWN

It is hardly possible to recount the college's evolving community role without reference to its Baptist ties.

A creature of the church, William Jewell nonetheless was secured for Liberty by forward-thinking citizens who were not overly concerned with theological distinctions. Thus, the college's location and ultimate success turned at least as much on the efforts of non-Baptist neighbors as it did on the support of the faithful throughout the state and, indeed, the nation.

In general, Baptists were late contestants in the race to plant colleges on America's expanding frontier. But as their numbers grew and their leaders weighed future prospects, Baptists entered the college business in earnest and eventually only the Presbyterians, Methodists and Catholics would establish more institutions of higher learning than the Baptists.

Until the late 1850s many within the denomination felt that their college was too close to the rough edges of nineteenth-century civilization. It was, in fact, a concerted effort by Clay County locals that resulted in a significant endowment for the college and, not incidentally, the sandbagging of the efforts of one Noah Flood who was bent on relocating the school to the mid or eastern—and more gentle—part of the state. So moved was he by this largesse that the Reverend Mr. Flood proclaimed: "Out of debt, out of debt. God must be in it, I surrender, and henceforth I am for William Jewell College at Liberty."

This was the second instance, and in some ways the most dramatic, of the community's support for the school. Perhaps as importantly, it clearly demonstrates that particularly in the early years the economic benefits of the town-gown marriage were not lost on either of the partners.

It is likely that Baptist influence in Liberty would have been rather substantial even without the college. But the presence of the school with its strong denominational ties and the natural bonding with local white Baptist congregations (of which the Second Baptist Church of Liberty has been the most significant) established a sectarian perspective with considerable and enduring impact upon the community. Even today, and not always fairly, those who appreciate the college and its religious tradition sometimes believe that influence has not always been helpful to the community's overall progress.

Prudently, those who framed the institution's charter made no provision for Baptist control. As Frank E. Atwood of the Missouri Supreme Court observed: "Whatever may be the reason for this omission, it is in favor of intellectual and religious freedom and is too conspicuous to have been unintentional." Intentional or not, this principle left administrators and trustees free to seek out a level of interaction with Missouri Baptists appropriate to the time and, more to the point, to the educational and intellectual mission of the college.

AT LIBERTY: AT HOME

Today William Jewell College is a part of a vibrant and diverse metropolitan community and serves a variety of worthwhile constituencies. But its most intimate relationship from the beginning has been with that little town that helped bring it about and that often, especially in the early years, did what was necessary to sustain the college and ensure its well-being.

One suspects that as long as William Jewell exists, its graduates will embrace the Liberty of their own time. Returning to it over the years, they will be moved and at the same time be regretful at its progress, but most will savor the bittersweet memories of the younger, less complicated time they walked its streets. The campus and town of memory become inseparable. Old grads easily forget how creative they were in avoiding the campus library. But to many, the old Plaza Theater, or the bowling alley, or the truck stop, or just an uncontested parking spot on the low road are perfected in time and become holy ground.

Early on, the presence of the college marked Liberty as a frontier town of promise. Though a fledgling village built in part by the rough river trade, Liberty had a grand vision of itself and thought a college an important ornament for a community on the move.

The new little college was expected to be set apart. The people who inhabited it were different and worried a lot about the improper influence sure to be found among the local townsfolk. So like many colleges of the time, William Jewell valued isolation and its founders were happy to find their school a home on one of Clay County's highest hills. There they enjoyed an aura of separation, and the eleva-

The old Plaza Theater was demolished in 1985 to make way for improvements to the Clay County Justice Center. Generations of William Jewell students mourned its passing.

tion provided an advantageous view of goings-on in Liberty, but at a safe distance.

On the whole, in its infancy William Jewell was not dissimilar to other colleges founded in the mid-nineteenth century. Contemporary handbooks discouraged students from too much time in town save for church attendance and, perhaps, other necessities. Youthful disregard could at times be consequential as when young Mr. Wiley was shot dead (some say by Jesse himself) as the James gang made its getaway from the famous Liberty Bank robbery. And a little later there was the other college in town. Doubtless, Liberty Ladies College, standing as it did on the commanding hill to the west, was a pervasive distraction to the hormonal young men on the other side of town. Fortunately, as we have seen, the town square was mostly off limits to students from both colleges and it stood impenetrable, a preserver of strong Victorian proprieties.

Unquestionably, the well-being of college and town have been inextricably bound since 1849. Nonetheless the relationship between the two has not always been particularly close and, at times, even strained. One graduate recalls a chapel talk by President Walter Pope Binns, an impassioned speech occasioned by a public altercation between two fraternities. "We may become a part of the town," Dr. Binns said. "We need to get along with those people. The police are old and we should not tax them with pranks of college students." While this grim perspective may have been shaped for effect, it does reflect a certain aloofness in college-town relations that prevailed well into the 1960s and early '70s.

In any college town community the annual tribal rites of undergraduates often shape attitudes. Traditional music and religious observances on the campus typically heightened the neighbors' enjoyment of the holiday season. Unfortunately, this good will could be offset for neighbors whose Scottish pines made excellent Christmas trees for fraternity house celebrations. And few flower gardens were safe in the late spring as the various Greek houses improved themselves for spring formals. These excesses eased as campus organizations began taking their formal events to local hotels; there was a marked improvement in community relations as a consequence. It is unlikely, though, that the campus and city hall could ever fully agree on matters of decorum. Typically, undergraduates are privileged and intelligent people whose mistakes are those of judgment, not intellect. Since it is good judgment that makes good neighbors, students occasionally cross over the line.

The influx of veterans following World War II forced dramatic change on college and university campuses across the country. They simply never were the same. Traditional prohibitions against drinking, dancing, and ribald behavior in general were largely ignored by young men (mostly, though some women) who, having confronted far greater temptation, thought themselves well beyond such

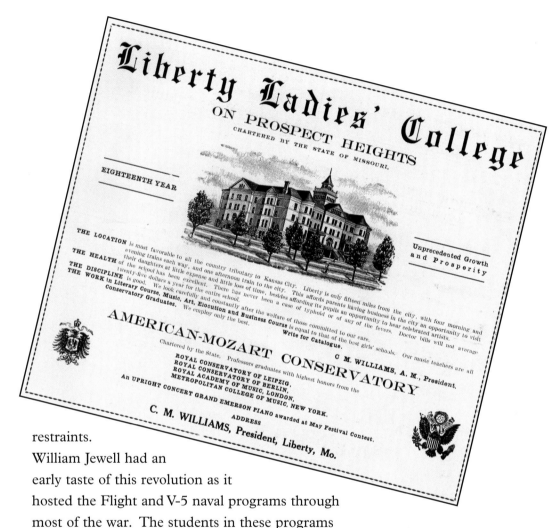

Liberty Ladies College

restraints. William Jewell had an early taste of this revolution as it hosted the Flight and V-5 naval programs through most of the war. The students in these programs reflected the maturity and seriousness of purpose that their post-war comrades would bring back to Liberty. Coeds, introduced at William Jewell just after World War I, sometimes were placed in fraternity houses to make room for the Navy men on campus. This brought instant improvement in neighborhood relations, but was a brush with scandal doubtless too close for some young women of the time.

City Hall, Liberty

The social awareness of students soon began to play a role in community relations. Even into the early 1960s Liberty was sharply segregated. Many who came to town were shocked to see "white only" public facilities and to learn that it was only after World War I that the United States flag, a symbol of deep division within the post-Civil War community, regained its prominence on the courthouse square. William Jewell students, like most students of the time, lacked an enlarged social conscience. That began to change dramatically in 1961 when Bill "Pee-Wee" Summers became the first full-time African-American student on the hill. His friends became aware of the inaccessibility of barbershops and the old Plaza Theater where blacks were relegated to the balcony. The presence of a popular and engaging African-American for the first time personalized that injustice for many students and they, though in small and different ways, influenced the community and eventually helped force an end to such overtly exclusionary practices.

It was also about this time that Liberty began the dramatic transformation that continues to this day. As a county seat, the town enjoyed a certain prominence that was not diminished by the larger justice center in Kansas City. Then, as now, a pantheon of keen business and legal minds was gathered around the county courthouse in the Liberty square. This included William Jewell men like Robert Sevier '30, Arthur Roy Kincaid '32, Bill Waters '37, and Francis Hale. College graduates were pillars on which the town square rested, with Art Reppert '38 to the north, Conn Withers '28 to the south and Garnett Peters '29, a major philanthropic force both on the campus and around the square, to the east. It is not surprising, then, that relationships forged in undergraduate days on the hill often became a building block for progress in the community.

As the town grew due to the post-war prosperity, its public officials were persons of substance and ability. The college's relationship with Liberty officials, especially with mayors and city administrators, strengthened substantially in the 1970s and subsequent decades. Liberty came of age attracting a series of very able mayors and professional administrators who led the town in times of extensive and remarkable change. Mayors such as Sam Carter '82, Russ Weathers, Glenna Todd, Robert Saunders, Bill Kersten, Steve Hawkins and city administrators Chuck Anderson, Lloyd Harrell '66, David Warm, and Gary Jackson had very different leadership styles but each was a person of vision with political acumen and the essential ability to enlist the community behind some truly monumental tasks. In 1997 yet another Jewell graduate, Stephen Arbo '84, took over as city administrator.

A series of events in the 1970s and the '80s will continue to shape Liberty's development well into the next century.

The Clay County Courthouse for years has occupied the city square and, both symbolically and economically, dominated the lives of Liberty citizens. Much of the business of the inner city hinged upon the presence of this and related facilities as well as the hundreds of persons who animated them.

It was the need to improve these facilities that precipitated one of the major crises in Liberty's history. There were those across Clay County who felt that the county as a whole would be better served if the justice center were pulled from the center of Liberty and placed on the town's edge. That, they claimed, would make county services more accessible and provide far greater convenience for those doing business at the county seat.

City leaders instantly recognized the potential for disintegration should the anchor business leave Liberty's town square. Other cities across the country were at risk as their central core eroded. Mobilizing as never before, and with the single-mindedness and tenacity seldom seen in communities of any size, Liberty fought for its very life. The college played a critical role in that effort.

Traditionally, college officials have been hesitant to involve the college in political initiatives of any sort. But that tradition was abandoned, for the moment at least, when President J. Gordon Kingsley testified at a public hearing before the Clay County Commission. There he presented compelling arguments for leaving the justice center in downtown Liberty. His speech made a difference. Later the presiding county commissioner admitted that Kingsley's testimony led him to cast his deciding vote in favor of the town square.

Things began to happen. First, a new city hall and municipal jail were constructed. Then, following a series of difficult but successful bond elections, the county's justice center and related facilities were built or refurbished, giving downtown Liberty an astonishing rebirth.

Had events gone differently, the viability of Liberty would be questionable. Fortunately, the will of Liberty citizens and the forcefulness of their leaders kept county justice facilities in place and rejuvenated Liberty—an unusually strong city, one whose future appears bright because its core industry remains in place. The benefits to the college, which from the very beginning lent unreserved support to the city and county efforts, are incalculable.

The college's direct financial contribution to Liberty is substantial. With an operating budget of over $25 million, William Jewell boasts a total economic impact of well over $80 million annually. Beyond that, the college's education programs and,

importantly, more than 5,000 graduates reside in and contribute to the economy of the larger metropolitan area.

The administration is alert to opportunities that will enhance the fiscal health of both the college and the community. In the early 1960s the Dallas Texans moved to Kansas City as the Kansas City Chiefs and for over thirty years the campus served as the summer home of the NFL franchise. Routinely, the campus provides facilities for a variety of skill camps. These and other events draw an estimated 140,000 people annually and visitors spend a significant amount of money in Liberty and the surrounding area.

While data can be used to demonstrate the magnitude of William Jewell's economic impact, they cannot adequately capture the college's formative role in helping to create within its host community a quality of life that is by any standard rare. It is difficult to imagine a Liberty without the cultural sustenance provided by the Liberty Symphony Orchestra, the Peters Theater, the Stocksdale Gallery and, more recently, the Grand River Chapel. The

Mabee Center for Physical Activity, completed in 1980, gave William Jewell students one of the finest facilities of its kind anywhere. Its swimming pool and indoor track are popular with all age segments in Liberty, and were especially important to the city's senior citizens prior to the construction of the new community center. And only five years later, College Place West, a twenty-home retirement development, was built on the northwest corner of the campus. Residents there have full access to campus facilities and programs and are able to participate to the extent they wish in virtually every aspect of college life. Other programs also serve to bring town and gown together to share the college's resources. Since 1953 the annual Science Night has attracted teachers and students from across the region. And, more recently, the new E.S. Pillsbury Observatory has offered a monthly Open House to provide community access to its 14-inch Celestron telescope.

Of special note in community relations is the work of the college's Woman's Committee. Over 200 members including alumnae, faculty, and friends support the college through a variety of projects, and its scholarship program offers three to four scholarships each year for deserving female students.

Few decisions are made on the Hill that do not take into account the feelings and needs of friends and neighbors in Liberty. The relationship between the town and its college generally has been congenial and, indisputably, mutually rewarding. The Clay

County Justice Center and Liberty Hospital bring immeasurable benefits to the city and its people. But it is likely that in generations to come Liberty will still be best known as the home of William Jewell College.

BUILDING A GREAT CITY

William Jewell's connections in Jackson County, especially those with the younger community that would become Kansas City, Mo., date to the college's earliest days when some of the area's leading families, bearing such names as Wornall, Pugh, and Reynolds, served as trustees and financial supporters.

Later other prominent families replaced them, but none has had more impact than Charles F. Curry. A realtor, developer, and banker, Curry served as a trustee from 1943 to 1968, half that span as board chair. His influence was felt long afterward through two business associates (and Jewell graduates), Carl Willard and Gene Moore, whom Curry brought to the college board.

These strong ties notwithstanding, until well after World War II the college struggled to define its role in the greater Kansas City community. This task was made more challenging because the college's image in the immediate region had been tainted from time to time by media accounts (fair or not) of internal conflict, sectarian bickering, and perhaps just imprudent management of public relations. But more damaging by far was the college's

relatively low profile and the general public's resulting ignorance of William Jewell's location and exceptional academic quality.

And then there was THE RIVER. Throughout the region's history the Missouri River has been one of the great divides of America's Midwest. Even with improved bridges and roadways, the river remained a significant psychological barrier, felt keenly by Kansas City's entire Northland region. To enhance its significance throughout the region, William Jewell had to deal head-on with this formidable obstacle.

The college's move center stage of metropolitan life was aided substantially by several forces. The most powerful was, and remains, the college's superb Fine Arts Program founded by Drs. Richard Harriman and Dean Dunham in 1965.

Founded in 1965, the Fine Arts Series gives William Jewell special status in metropolitan Kansas City. Here, director Richard Harriman, is shown with donors Beth and Bob Ingram.

Former presidential candidate Michael Dukakis visits with students at William Jewell in 1993.

Walter Pope Binns with President Lyndon B. Johnson

Thomas Coleman '65 served Missouri's 6th District in the U.S. House of Representatives for sixteen years.

President Chris Sizemore has emphasized the importance of information technology and carried this into the community. Here (left) he appears with other leaders in "Liberty Links," a cooperative venture between the college and community that capitalizes on emerging technologies.

Its standing among campus-based performing arts programs rarely disputed, the William Jewell series brings affordable access to the leading performing artists of the time. The greater Kansas City area has come to embrace the William Jewell Fine Arts Program and Dr. Harriman as their own. The halo effect of their excellence has, perhaps more than any other factor, enhanced the prestige and visibility of the entire college.

Achievement Day, the invention of Professor P. Casper Harvey, was begun in 1944 as a platform for recognizing outstanding William Jewell graduates. The format calls for an annual speaker of national or international note. This feature has expanded the event's appeal to the general public.

Through the years Achievement Day honorees have done a great deal to define the college in the public eye and to raise its profile as a significant community resource.

It is not surprising that graduates who have achieved unusual prominence in their fields have also shaped the college's standing. At least three William Jewell alumni served the United States Congress during the twentieth century. Representative Clarence Cannon was by far the most prominent, for it was he who eventually chaired the powerful House Ways and Means Committee. Representative Pat Williams '63 was elected to Congress in 1976 where he served for almost twenty years. Also entering Congress that year was E. Thomas Coleman, a 1965 graduate who had served in the state legislature and as an assistant attorney general for the state of Missouri. William Jewell graduates in Missouri's Sixth Congressional District were proud to have one of their own sitting in Congress, and anyone or anything related to William Jewell was always afforded special attention when visiting the congressman's Washington office.

The list of other public servants related to the college over the past half century is long and distinguished. It includes Missouri Supreme Court Justice Al Rendlen '41, Missouri Court of Appeals Judges Robert Ulrich '63 and William E. Turnage '47, and individuals such as A.J. Wilson '63, city manager of Kansas City, and Dennis

Lambert '63, who became minority staff director of the House Committee on Agriculture.

Of special note is the contribution of Anita McPike Gorman '53, who became the champion of the Northland area and later a leader throughout Kansas City and the state. A person of incredible will, she has been a gentle but irresistible force in promoting interest in Kansas City's Northland and always in her alma mater. Her imprimatur made it comfortable for others, non-Baptists, non-William Jewell people, to become enthusiastic about the college's prospects and to support its programs. Mrs. Gorman now serves on the college's board of trustees.

These and so many other William Jewell people enhanced the college's reputation through their own performance and most could be counted upon to assist the college in every appropriate way.

At one time or another virtually every member of the college community has the opportunity to help determine William Jewell's image. But it is the president who bears the primary responsibility for shaping how its contemporary publics view the institution.

Over the last half of the twentieth century, variously talented men of integrity have served William Jewell as president. Inevitably, the college's relations with the community have tended to reflect the personality and leadership style of the sitting president.

When he came to the office, Walter Pope Binns

Anita McPike Gorman

brought an imperial bearing and a powerful presence—unusual even at a time when those attributes were considered attractive in a college president. Indeed, it is likely that it was his courtly, aloof demeanor that caused the college's trustees to seek him out; they would, he later observed, overlook his propensity for black cigars and perhaps even appreciate his habit of wearing white linen suits while bass fishing. Neither were they concerned that the Binns' Cadillac seldom acknowledged stop signs in Liberty, and that friends and neighbors were careful to give it a wide berth.

Dr. Binns was a profoundly sensitive man who always placed first the needs of the college and the community that it served. However, he carried with him from Virginia the traditional view that college and community were best held at arm's length from each other, and he seemed always suspicious of the big city and the mischief he knew was possible

159

1986 Yates Medalists included (from left) Anita B. Gorman, James M. Kemper, Jr., Josph T. McGuff, President J. Gordon Kingsley, Mary Prichard, Frank White, Jr. and John F. Prichard, Jr.

there. As a result, he did not consider it particularly important to position the college more advantageously in the greater metropolitan area; in fact, he saw its relative geographical isolation as one of William Jewell's chief assets. He himself was well known and highly regarded by leaders in the city and across the country. As *The Kansas City Star* opined at his death, "He was always the quiet, considerate southern gentleman in the best sense of the term. Many persons in Kansas City which had no connection with either the college or the Baptist faith will recall Dr. Binns for his fine addresses to civic and religious groups." And tellingly, the same writer continued, "His real contribution was on the William Jewell campus where the Binns era left an indelible mark on one of the fine small colleges in the Middle West."

H. Guy Moore came to the presidency having held the pulpit of the prestigious Wornall Road Baptist Church in Kansas City. There he had established good relations with some of the city's most influential people, a few of whom served the college as trustees. It was disappointing to many that his tenure lasted only a few years and, as a conse-

quence, his impact on the college's position in the community was minimal. However, students viewed him with genuine affection, and especially appreciated Mrs. Myron Moore who opened the President's Home to both campus and community and made it a familiar and yet always special place for undergraduates to visit.

The two years subsequent to Dr. Moore's resignation in 1968 were difficult and did very little to enhance William Jewell's standing within the community. While the college was without a permanent president, the dissent that was then buffeting all of America's higher education institutions reached Liberty. But friends in the Kansas City area were probably more amused than alarmed when a small group of students, taking up the cause of a terminated professor, predicted the school's demise because beer could not be consumed in Greene Stadium and certain four-letter words were prohibited in the classroom. Fortunately, Dr. E.W. Holzapfel, long a mainstay of the college, emerged as acting president and restored a sense of decorum and self-confidence.

This prepared the way for the administration of Thomas S. Field, who came to the college in 1970, the fourth president for those seniors who would graduate in the class of 1971. A gregarious and self-confident man, President Field was an excellent representative for the college, a good public speaker, and always dressed immaculately. Not a professional educator, he prudently relied heavily upon his staff and deferred to faculty colleagues on issues of educational programming. Under his leadership an initiative called "Achievement '70s" reshaped the college's curriculum and extracurricular programs and laid the groundwork for William Jewell's emergence as a regional leader in higher education.

Dr. and Mrs. Field enhanced the President's Home as a center for both campus and community events. As in all things related to the school, the discerning and cultured taste of Virginia Field was ever apparent.

Of course, every college president has to ask for money from time to time. Tom Field was the first to hire a director of development and make fund raising an integral part of the college's administration. He was by nature an effective salesman and that skill did much to promote William Jewell throughout the business and philanthropic communities. Pillsbury Music Center, Mabee Center for Physical Activities, and the Binns Lectureship are legacies of the Field administration. But it was the Mabee Center that was "his" project, one that was born largely out of his enthusiasm and his ability to persuade trustees. The center stands even today as a symbol of his commitment to the college and its larger community.

The emergence of J. Gordon Kingsley as the college's president in 1979 was a watershed in William Jewell's long struggle to define itself within the metropolitan area. Trained in both theology and literature, Kingsley was the first William Jewell president in modern times to come from the professoriate and this perspective distinguished him from his immediate predecessors. He had a much broader vision of William Jewell's educational mission, one that called for a greatly enhanced role in the affairs of the metropolitan area. He was, for the quiet little college in Liberty, a revolution in presidential leadership: intellectually astute, open, engaging, charming, playfully irreverent, and with a wonderful talent for not taking himself too seriously.

President Gordon Kingsley

Kingsley sensed the possibilities. He was alert to new trends and began building strategies to position the college as Kansas City's own. He was aided in this effort by the appeal of the college's Fine Arts Series, especially among financial and cultural leaders and through carefully orchestrated appearances that placed him before the Kansas City elite. He skillfully exploited Fine Arts activities, events like "The City Come Again" Christmas service at Grace and Holy Trinity Cathedral, and luncheon talks before the leading service groups in the city soon made him the most visible and sought-after college president in the metropolitan area.

Kingsley was gifted at constructing pithy, memorable capsules, repeating them frequently, and gearing them to his audiences. Soon people believed. He was a critical, indeed the essential, element in the college's emergence in the 1980s as the premier liberal arts school in the Kansas City region. With his enhanced visibility came incremental growth in philanthropic support from the leading foundations and individuals of the region. The generosity of the Hall Family Foundations and Muriel Kauffman's endowment for the Fine Arts Series are compelling evidence of Kingsley's unprecedented access to Kansas City's civic and philanthropic leadership.

President Kingsley's untimely resignation in 1993 took a heavy toll on the gains within the community that the college had made under his leadership. Even so, the William Jewell story was out and most within the larger community, though lamenting Kingsley's absence, understood the treasure that is the college in Liberty.

This insight did much to assist President W. Christian Sizemore when he assumed William Jewell's presidency in the summer of 1994. Asserting his own educational perspective, President Sizemore made community relations a major priority. Soon after arriving in Liberty he took a seat on the board of the Liberty Chamber of Commerce and the Clay County Development Commission. While other college officers had previously been active in these organizations, Sizemore was the first of William Jewell's presidents to serve these important community functions. His influence was also felt in expanding the membership of the board of trustees to include non-Baptist alumni and other business and professional leaders, as well as including faculty and student members on trustee committees. His wife, Anne Sizemore, has also helped mold the college's image under her husband's leadership. The President's Home is again central to undergraduate life and an elegant focal point for alumni and community interaction.

As the future unfolds into a new millennium, William Jewell College has earned an enviable reputation as a quality institution that has served its community well. Such privilege brings with it a sense of fragility and an awareness that it must be earned in every generation.

We wish her well, those of us who owe so much to the little college on the Hill.

CHAPTER 12

JEWELL 2000

We Will Love Thee, Praise Thee Forever

by W. Christian Sizemore

*T*he sesquicentennial of William Jewell College provides unique opportunity to celebrate and honor the past, experience the present, and anticipate and invest in the future. This is a time to remember those who have given of themselves to make William Jewell a quality institution that has focused on the importance of value-centered education.

A revealing story is told about John Stewart Mill, the great English philosopher and economist of the nineteenth century. It is said that early one morning, Mill awoke with a strange and over-whelming feeling—in his words, a sense that "the answer to the question of the ages" had come to him sometime in the middle of the night. But, try as he might, Mill could not remember what the answer was.

So, the following night, he placed a pen and a sheet of paper on the table next to his bed. A few mornings later when he awoke with the same feel-ing, Mill looked at the paper and found—in his own handwriting—the simple phrase, "Think in different terms."

For 150 years William Jewell College has

> *"We may not live in the past, but the past lives in us. We should know our history. The people that despise their past are ignoble and there is no hope for them in the future; and the people that are ignorant of their past will not only make great blunders, but must also lack courage and inspiration in present and future struggles."*
>
> —John Priest Greene

enjoyed the benefits that accrue to those willing to think in different terms. Because the leadership, including the board of trustees and faculty, has been willing to think in different terms, William Jewell has successfully met the challenges of change for a century and a half. With a solid base of accomplishments, the college approaches the twen-ty-first century with unparalleled opportunities as one of the nation's leading liberal arts colleges that features both strong academics and strong Christian identity.

As our world approaches the year 2000, there is growing excitement about the idea that we will be experiencing a rare, historical moment with the

Dr. W. Christian Sizemore has made academic quality a cornerstone of strategic planning. He is shown here on the quad with Dr. Nina T. Pollard, provost and vise president for academic affairs, who was recruited in 1997 to provide new leadership for Jewell's many academic initiatives.

conclusion of a century and the birth of a new millennium. This pivotal moment coincides with the sesqui-centennial anniversary of William Jewell College, thus providing us with the perfect opportunity to reflect on where we have been, on who we are, and what we hope to become.

The basis of the core mission of William Jewell College has always been a broad background in the liberal arts. The liberal arts provide the basis for leadership, and leadership is a performing art that requires communicating clearly, solving problems, making rational decisions, living ethically, rendering service, and accommodating change. The liberal arts will continue to be the best preparation for a rapidly changing world.

Every generation has noted the changes and challenges which it faces, but our generation is confronted with the most radical rate of change in history. In addition, the dawning of a new millennium symbolizes the dramatic impact of technology and globalization on our present and our future. In the midst of this change, a strong liberal arts-based education like that provided by William Jewell College is especially important. This type of educa-

tion, more than any other, provides a student the background to continue to learn and to assimilate change.

With today's amazing advances in transportation and communication, we are prone to point out how much smaller the world has become. Indeed, this has always been a small world, and its future will continue to be shaped by individuals of strength, character, and vision like William Jewell and Alexander Doniphan. Their dedication and leadership created William Jewell, aided by hundreds of trustees, faculty, and alumni leaders who have sustained William Jewell College as an institution of quality.

In the next century William Jewell and its counterparts will focus intently on the goal of creating and sustaining quality, for it is this characteristic more than any other that will enable higher education to meet the needs of our society. Creative, quality education encompasses efforts to help a person develop spiritually, socially, morally, and physically, as well as intellectually.

Our mission statement calls for William Jewell College to:

1. Provide students a liberal arts education of superior quality,

2. Serve communities beyond the campus educationally, culturally, and socially,

3. Be an institution loyal to the ideals of

Christ, demonstrating a Christian philosophy for the whole of life, and expressing the Missouri Baptist heritage which is the foundation of the College.

Elton Trueblood, a modern prophet who has often called our generation back to the real values, reminds us that, "the only reasonable way to judge a college is not by the size of its campus or by the abundance of its financial resources or by the number of books in its library or even by the publications of its professors. The college is to be judged by the quality of its human product. The test of a successful college education is not to be found in the amount of knowledge which graduates take away with them, most of which will be forgotten in any case, but rather by the appetite to know, by the determination to continue the educational process, and by the ability to think and act maturely. The purpose of a college is the production of persons who are both more civilized and more civilizing."

As we prepare for the twenty-first century, there is no shortage of futurists predicting the many changes we may expect to see first. Predicting the future is a precarious endeavor, and the truth, of course, is that no one knows. However, we know that technology is increasingly important to our present and our future. William Jewell College and all institutions of quality must incorporate the tools of technology, communications, and transportation

in order to meet the challenges of our rapidly changing global community.

The college's future will include increasing emphasis on the teaching of leadership, global citizenship, ethics, and spiritual values which will augment William Jewell's already strong liberal arts foundation. The future also requires a cohesive education program that involves students actively in the teaching-learning-serving process. The leadership of William Jewell will meet the challenge of providing financial and physical resources adequate to sustain this vital mission.

A few years ago a research study predicted that early in the new millennium our nation's colleges and universities would appear more and more alike, pressed into conformity by declining resources and a headlong rush to be a part of the herd. There is no question in my mind that William Jewell College will avoid this destiny. We will continue to fulfill our legacy and achieve our true mission through an unashamed emphasis on values and an unrelenting quest for quality. Values and quality, in short, will ensure that William Jewell maintains its integrity and its distinction while meeting the needs of a global society in a rapidly changing world.

The twenty-first century will be called the "age of creativity" and the "age of imagination" and the "age of information." Capitalizing on this new age of enlightenment will require the same pioneer spirit

Dr. W. Christian Sizemore assumed the top leadership role at William Jewell in 1994. His initial priority was formulating a sound strategic plan to guide institutional decision-making and re-positioning Jewell as one of the most competitive liberal arts colleges of its type.

that empowered Jewell and Doniphan to establish a college on the nation's frontier 150 years ago. In the twenty-first century we will be pushing to new frontiers, reaching across disciplinary boundaries, and reinventing the future.

The College motto, "Deo Fisus Labora," is translated "Trust in God and Work." Inspired by this motto, the leadership of William Jewell College has attained inspiring achievements during its first 150 years. With broad-based support from all of its current constituents, William Jewell will continue to be a national model for educational leadership and service. *Deo Fisus Labora.*

ABOUT THE AUTHORS

Donald J. Hall

Foreword

B.A., Dartmouth College

Donald J. Hall serves as chairman of the board for Hallmark Cards, Inc. the famed greeting card company founded by his father, Joyce C. Hall, 88 years ago. After graduating from Dartmouth College, Hall joined the U.S. Army, serving most of his military career as an officer at a small post in Gifu, Japan. His career at Hallmark has included service as assistant to the president, administrative vice president, president and chief executive officer. He stepped down as CEO in 1986, but still serves as chairman of the company and provides leadership to numerous civic and philanthropic organizations in greater Kansas City.

As the scion of a famous family with deep roots in Kansas City, Hall has a unique perspective on William Jewell's "town and gown" connection. In reflecting on how the history of Jewell and Kansas City have intertwined for 150 years, Hall says he gained "a deep appreciation for Jewell's tremendous impact on the Kansas City region—both in educating civic and professional leaders and in offering cultural programs to the city at large." The college, he says, "is one of the assets that makes Kansas City so special."

David O. Moore

Chapter One: History of William Jewell

B.A. Ouachita University; Th.M., Ph.D., Southern Seminary

Dr. David O. Moore served as professor and chair of the religion department from 1956 to 1986. He remains active in the life of the college by visiting with faculty colleagues and alumni, attending athletic and cultural events, and maintaining trustee friendships. To research his chapter, he spent well over a year surveying past issues of the college newspaper, trustee minutes, and various writings about the college.

After completing his research efforts, Moore commented, "One sees in the study of this history the tremendous growth of Jewell in the era of the last half-century. I enjoyed re-living the great number of experiences that have helped Jewell become a better college."

Doran McCarty

Chapter Two: Christian Heritage

B.A. William Jewell College; B.D., Ph.D., Southern Seminary

Doran McCarty '52 is president of McCarty Services, a not-for-profit organization that offers training seminars for ministers. He served as a pastor of churches in Missouri, Kentucky, and Indiana, and was a faculty member of Midwestern Baptist Theological Seminary and Golden Gate Theological Seminary. He started the Northeastern Baptist School of Ministry, with a main office in New York City and branch offices in Boston, Baltimore, and Pittsburgh, and was executive director of Seminary Extension out of Nashville, Tenn.

Dr. McCarty enjoyed reviewing William Jewell's religious impact. "The college's spiritual legacy is providing an atmosphere where individuals can have a moving religious experience and encounter God. William Jewell allows students to maintain their religious interests in a refreshing manner."

Jerry Cain

Chapter Three: Campus Buildings

B.S. Eastern New Mexico University; M.A. Baylor University; additional studies at Midwestern Baptist Theological Seminary, St. Paul School of Theology, Oxford University

Currently president of Judson College in Elgin, Ill., Jerry Cain served William Jewell College for 20 years as college chaplain; in 1985 he was named collegiate vice president. A well-known preacher and teacher, Dr. Cain left a legacy of student servants and service learning at William Jewell.

In reviewing the history of campus buildings, he learned that "books and bricks serve as lasting legacies to heroes of the past who wanted to provide teaching tools for professors and students of the present generation."

Myra Unger

Chapter Four: Faculty and Administration

B.A. William Jewell College;
M.A. Washington University;
Ed.D. University of Kansas

Myra Unger '60, professor of English Emerita at William Jewell, served as a member of the William Jewell faculty from 1961 to 1994. Currently, she is a freelance writer and community volunteer. Three of her sons graduated from William Jewell: Roy Cozad '76, Scott Cozad '77, and Kanon Cozad '92. She and her husband, Brian '73, have a son, Blair, who is to graduate from high school in 1999.

In working on this project, Dr. Unger was reminded of how crucial faculty members are, both to a college's educational mission and to students' individual lives. "As Henry Adams said, 'A teacher affects eternity.'"

Neita Geilker

Chapter Five: Student Life

B.A. William Jewell College;
Ed.M. Harvard Graduate
School of Education; Ph.D.
University of Missouri
Kansas City

Neita Geilker '56 is a
"grammar guru," teaching communication skills as a trainer,
consultant, and professional speaker with her own company,
Geilker and Associates. She was an adjunct instructor in
Jewell's English department for 20 years. She is married to
William Jewell physics professor Don Geilker '55 and is the
mother of Jewell graduates Emily '82 and Eric '85.

Working on this project allowed her to take a stroll down
memory lane: "I thoroughly enjoyed contacting a wide array
of alumni to gather information about their activities and
memories of college days; I also enjoyed the excuse to wander
through many old yearbooks, both to reminisce and to
encounter amazing insights about college life in other eras."

Ann Marie Shannon

Chapter Six: Academics

B.A. Agnes Scott College; A.M.
Radcliffe College-Harvard
University; Ph.D. Emory
University

As assistant to the president
for planning, Ann Marie Shannon guided the college through
two years of intensive reflection and goal-setting during the
1996-97 strategic planning process. In addition, she has served
William Jewell as a professor of English, associate dean,
Oxbridge senior tutor, "Foundations" program coordinator and
overseas study coordinator. Currently, she is enjoying retirement.

As she prepared to write the chapter on academics, she
especially enjoyed "studying old catalogs and reports to trace
both continuity and change in the college's understanding of
itself and of what it could offer its students."

Norris Patterson

Chapter Seven: Cardinal Athletics

B.S. Missouri Valley College; M.A. University of Missouri
Kansas City; Ed.D. Columbia University

Before beginning his legendary run as Jewell's most successful head football coach with 13 conference championships,
Norris Patterson served five years in the U.S. Navy in Europe
during World War II and was discharged as
Lieutenant Commander in 1946. His long
tenure at William Jewell began in 1950 when
he was named department chair and head
football coach, a post in which he served until
1968. He returned to Jewell to chair the
department from 1975 to 1989.

Norris Patterson, author of *A Century of
Cardinal Sports*, is considered the reigning
authority on William Jewell athletics. He says
he enjoyed the opportunity to research Jewell's post-war athletic
history in greater detail. "I enjoyed reviewing this period of
history—about 40 of theses years were mine, so it was fun.
Seeing the changes over the years amazed me."

D. Dean Dunham, Jr.

Chapter Eight: Fine Arts Program

B.A. Hastings College; M.A. University of Arkansas
Fayetteville; Ph.D. University of Nebraska Lincoln

Dr. Dean Dunham, who has taught English at William
Jewell for 33 years, co-founded the William Jewell College Fine
Arts Program along with fellow English professor Richard
Harriman. More than 30 years ago, the duo recognized a need
among fine arts patrons in Kansas City for a program to bring
acclaimed artists to the city. What began with a couple of events

has blossomed into one of the Midwest's finest
series, annually bringing to campus such artists as
Luciano Pavarotti, Itzhak Perlman, the American
Ballet Theatre, and The King's Singers.

"Richard and I saw the need for our students
to gain access to the performing arts. Under
Richard's guiding hand, the program has grown
into something beyond our expectations," he says.
"Writing this chapter on the Fine Arts Program
gave me occasion to celebrate two things: the
college's opportunity to create an extraordinary educational
program, and the success of a valued colleague in making the
most of that opportunity."

Georgia Bowman

Chapter Nine:
Women at William Jewell

B.A. William Jewell College; B.J.
School of Journalism, University
of Missouri Columbia; M.A.,
Ph.D. University of Iowa.

Dr. Georgia Bowman '34
edited two quarterly journals and wrote a brief monograph,
The Distaff Side, chronicling the history of women at William
Jewell. A fixture of the William Jewell faculty for 40 years, she
served as director of forensics, supervisor of the *Student* and
the *Tatler*, manager of the college radio station, and chair of the
department of communication. The annual first-year student
speech contest is named in her honor. For six years she was a
member of the alumni board of governors.

Dr. Bowman had but one regret in writing her chapter:
not enough space. "My reaction to developing the chapter on
women brought both joy and frustration because space limitations necessitated omitting material on so many women who
have contributed so much to the college."

John F. Truex and Kit Truex Mair

Chapter Ten: Greek Life

John F. Truex

B.A. William Jewell College; M.A. Northwestern University;
Ph.D. Stanford University

The Truex connection to William Jewell dates back to 1880 when John Truex's uncle Harvey came to the Hill. In all, 13 members of the Truex family have been William Jewell students. John '47, who was an active member of the Kappa Alpha fraternity, has served the college as a trustee and trustee emeritus as well as president of the national alumni association. He spent 34 years with TWA, eventually as a corporate vice president. For the last 17 years, he has been a consultant for the executive search firm Morton, McCorkle and Associates.

For John Truex, the best part of this project proved to be gaining new insights. "This project enhanced my knowledge of the various Greek organizations–their ideals and the significant contributions of each chapter and alumni."

Kit Truex Mair

B.A. William Jewell College

Kit Truex Mair '77 is the 12th member of the Truex family to attend William Jewell College. During her years at William Jewell, she was involved with many campus organizations, especially the sorority Zeta Tau Alpha. Professionally, she has worked in the fields of education, government and business, including 13 years at Marion Merrell Dow. Currently, she is a business consultant and a distributor for The Peoples Network.

"The Truex family is truly an inter-fraternity family, with six different Greek organizations represented through the generations," she says. "Helping to write this chapter with my father was fun and has raised my appreciation and awareness of the role each fraternity and sorority has played in people's lives."

Daniel Lambert

Chapter Eleven: Jewell and Community

B.A. William Jewell College; M.A. Northwestern University; Ph.D. University of Missouri-Columbia

Dr. Lambert '63 enjoyed a long career with William Jewell College, serving as dean of student affairs, executive assistant to the president, vice president for planning and development, and finally as vice president of the college. Since 1987 he has been president of Baker University in Baldwin City, Kan., along with his wife, Carolyn '65.

He approached this project with both joy and sorrow: "The college whose history this is, very early helped shape my life. The opportunity to tell some of its story has been a rare, if at times melancholy, privilege. Walking through the memories of youth is always a bit sad." He believes the college's greatest contribution to the community is as an intellectual and cultural force.

W. Christian Sizemore

Chapter Twelve: Jewell 2000

B.A. University of Richmond; B.D. Southeastern Baptist Theological Seminary; M.S.L.S. University of North Carolina; Ph.D. Florida State University.

Dr. W. Christian Sizemore assumed the presidency of William Jewell in 1994, after a lengthy career as a college president, chief academic officer, and professor. A native Virginian whose academic specialty is library science, Dr. Sizemore also has a divinity degree and long history of involvement in Baptist leadership and church relations.

As a student of William Jewell history, he was "amazed and impressed" at the variety of facts and anecdotes that surfaced during the compilation of this book. Also, he says, "It was an honor for me to articulate a vision for William Jewell's future. The college's history and traditions provide a magnificent basis for future success. Nothing but great things lie ahead, and I am excited to be a part of this continuing, distinctive and compelling story."

Juarenne Hester

Chair, Sesquicentennial Committee

B.A. William Jewell College; M.A. University of Missouri-Kansas City

Juarenne Hester '55 is currently one of Liberty's most active community volunteers. An English teacher in the Liberty public schools for 34 years, she was a finalist in Missouri's statewide "teacher of the year" recognition program. Since leaving the classroom, she has been active promoting bond and levy campaigns to benefit the local schools. At William Jewell she has been a part-time instructor, an officer of the alumni board of governors and co-chair of the alumni board's communications commission.

As chair of the Sesquicentennial Committee, a community-wide group comprised of several dozen civic and educational leaders, Mrs. Hester devoted countless hours to ensuring proper recognition for the college's 150th observance. This book, a key component of that celebration, was made more affordable to alumni and friends due to a generous gift from Juarenne Hester. The book is dedicated to her late husband, Frank Hester.

Mrs. Hester took an active interest in updating Jewell's history because of her profound love for the college. "William Jewell really nourished me as a person, and I want to do my part to ensure a quality educational experience for all who come in future years. I am confident that the next 150 years will be as interesting and inspiring as those chronicled in these pages."

John Young

Chair, Sesquicentennial Publications and Historical Research Committee

B.A. William Jewell College; M.A.L.S. University of Denver; M.P.A. University of Missouri Kansas City.

John Young '64 serves the college as assistant professor and director of Curry Library. He began his career with William Jewell's library in the summer of 1964, less than a month after graduation. He started at the circulation desk and moved through various staff positions in the former Carnegie Library and then to the new Charles F. Curry Library, assuming the position of director of the library in March of 1969.

He says working on this project made him feel "connected" to William Jewell history in a more meaningful way. "Being a part of the process of recording memories, and working closely with the authors, made me feel like I too was becoming a part of that history."

Raymond C. Jones

Editorial Coordinator, Sesquicentennial Publications and Historical Research Committee

B.A. Dickinson College; M.S. University of Illinois; Graduate Diploma, Johns Hopkins School for Advanced International Studies.

Raymond C. Jones, executive director of college relations at William Jewell, took over as book coordinator when Jerry Cain assumed the presidency of Judson College. Before coming to William Jewell in 1997 he had a lengthy career in the newspaper business, and also served as the top public relations official at Winthrop University, Monmouth University and Dickinson College.

He enjoyed this project because it provided a "fast learning curve" on the history of his newly adopted college. "I enjoyed working with the authors, and was impressed by both the depth of their knowledge and their extraordinary loyalty to William Jewell."

Charles Durbin
Editor, Cardinal Is Her Color

B.A. William Jewell College

As a student, Charles Durbin '60 served as editor of the *Student*, which was later renamed the *Hilltop Monitor*. During his tenure, the paper changed from a semi-monthly publication to a weekly one. His youngest daughter, Monica Cross, graduated from Jewell in 1990.

During the last 38 years, he has been the mortgage vice president and assistant secretary in the investment department at Business Men's Assurance Company. His hobbies include photography, particularly wedding pictures, and he put that talent to use in the pages of this book.

"I anticipated that a project of this nature would be challenging yet rewarding, and the high level of cooperation, enthusiasm and responsiveness has proved this true. I must thank my bride of 38 years, Judy, for helping me in the editing, review and opinion process and for offering constant support.

"The authors have invested much time and talent in the creation of these pages and they are truly remarkable people. The information herein is revealing of the many facets of life at William Jewell, and the vast number of Jewell connections which have been woven throughout this country and indeed the world in 150 years."